T0380436

ENGLISH CAMP
THAILAND

Marco Bussanich

ENGLISH CAMP THAILAND

iUniverse books may be ordered through booksellers or by contacting:

iUniverse
1663 Liberty Drive
Bloomington, IN 47403
www.iuniverse.com
1-800-Authors (1-800-288-4677)

ISBN: 978-1-5320-3679-8 (sc)
ISBN: 978-1-5320-3678-1 (e)

Library of Congress Control Number: 2017917230

Print information available on the last page.

iUniverse rev. date: 02/05/2018

Contents

Beginners—Lessons B1–B14

Intermediate—Lessons I1-I14

Advanced—Lessons A1-A14

Contents—Detailed

B—Beginners   I—Intermediate   A—Advanced

B6	Thai Marine Life	
Grammar	**Vocabulary**	**Focus**
Prepositions	Above, behind, below, from, front, between, next to, on, out of, on top of, under, close to	Use prepositions to describe positions of Thai marine life

B7	Thai Marine Life	
Grammar	**Vocabulary**	**Focus**
Nouns Contractions	Names of Thai fruits Contractions for the words: I, he, she, it, we, they	Use contractions to describe Thai fruits

B1	Elephants, Whales, and Dolphins	
Skill	**Action**	**Pages**
Reading/Writing	Examine animal diagram and body parts. Match body parts to correct column.	1
Speaking	Students pair up. Ask each other questions on how to express dimensions as both a noun and adjective (pages 7, 9, and 11). Partner responds. Reverse roles.	

B2	Describing Thai Marine Life	
Skill	**Action**	**Pages**
Writing **Speaking**	Use adjectives (classified as determiners, size and shape, observation, and color) to write descriptive sentences about Thai marine life. Pair up with a partner. Using sentences you wrote, read them out to your partner. Then reverse roles.	12

B3	Thai Kids	
Skill	**Action**	**Pages**
Reading Writing **Speaking**	Understand pronoun gender and number. Write correct pronoun in sentences. Students pair up and read sentences out loud.	18

Grammar	Vocabulary	Focus
The Verb "To Be" Present Simple Present Continuous	Is, are, was, were, am	Be, present simple, present continuous Describe actions of elephants

B12	Thai People and Their Customs	
Grammar	**Vocabulary**	**Focus**
Adverbs of Frequency	Always, almost always, often, usually, sometimes, seldom, occasionally, rarely, never	Describe Thai people with adverbs of frequency

B13	Questions about Thailand	
Grammar	**Vocabulary**	**Focus**
"Wh" Questions	Who, whose, where, when, which, what, why, how	Make "wh" questions from an answer

B14	Thai Kids at the Beach	
Grammar	**Vocabulary**	**Focus**
Simple Present Present Continuous **Subject/Verb Agreement**	Is, are, was, were, am	Correctly use "to be," present simple, present continuous, and subject/verb agreement

I1	My Holiday in Phuket	
Grammar	**Vocabulary**	**Focus**
Expressions of Time Past, Present, and Future Verbs	Previous, present, and past; expressions of time	Change verb tense from present tense, to either past tense or future tense
	Numerous verbs in past, present, and future tenses	

B8	1—Kids and the Environment: Saving Thailand's Oceans 2—Recycling, Reusing, and Saving Power	
Skill	**Action**	**Pages**
Writing Reading	Choose the correct synonym. Read (1) new words and (2) two stories.	39

I2	A Day at the Beach	
Grammar	**Vocabulary**	**Focus**
Present Simple Present Continuous	Numerous verbs will be studied in the present simple and present continuous tenses	Choose correct verb in the present simple and present continuous
I3	Geographical Use of the Word "The"	
Grammar	**Vocabulary**	**Focus**
The	The, geographical nouns	Choose if "the" belongs with a word
I4	Eating Thai Food	
Grammar	**Vocabulary**	**Focus**
Regular and Irregular Verbs	Many regular and irregular verbs in the present and past tense	Change verbs from present to past tense
I5	At Safari World	
Grammar	**Vocabulary**	**Focus**
Conjunctions	And, or, so, and many other conjunctions	Use conjunctions to connect two sentences
I6	Riding and Feeding Elephants in Ayuttyaha	
Grammar	**Vocabulary**	**Focus**
Verb Tenses	Regular and irregular verbs for feeding and riding elephants	Change the verb from present to past tense
I7	Tribal Shamans and Spiritual Healers	
Grammar	**Vocabulary**	**Focus**
Prepositions	Many single-word prepositions will be used	Choose prepositions in sentences
Prepositional Phrases	**Preposition + noun phrase**	Determine if word is a preposition or adverb
I8	The Thai Jungle	
Grammar	**Vocabulary**	**Focus**
Action and State of Being Verbs	A number of action and state of being verbs will be used	Write action and state of being verbs

A6	Sukhothai and Ayuttyaha: Thailand's Ancient Capitals	
Skill	**Action**	**Pages**
Compound Words	Read a story. Write compound words next to their definitions.	158

A7	Tsunami from the 2005 Indian Ocean Earthquake	
Grammar	**Vocabulary**	**Focus**
Phrasal Verbs	Twelve phrasal verbs	Place phrasal verbs correctly in a story

A8	Thai Cities, Towns, and Islands	
Grammar	**Vocabulary**	**Focus**
Adjective Clauses	Various adjectives and that, who, which, and whose	Make two sentences into one with adjective clauses

A9	Animism and Rituals in Thai Life	
Grammar	**Vocabulary**	**Focus**
Phrasal Verbs	Seventeen phrasal verbs	Place phrasal verbs correctly in a story

A10	Hotel Phuket	
Grammar	**Vocabulary**	**Focus**
Conversation	Nouns, verbs, and is, are, does, do, how, whom, where, which	Practice conversation with given vocabulary

A11	Thai History	
Grammar	**Vocabulary**	**Focus**
Present Perfect **Present Perfect** **Continuous**	For, since Many other verbs	Study past actions that continue into the present

A12	Motorcycles and Transportation in Thailand	
Grammar	**Vocabulary**	**Focus**
Compound Words	Numerous compound words	Learn compound words in a story

Introduction

This book is the first in a series of English-language books based on a number of different countries, specifically those in Southeast Asia and Latin America. The goal is to use the histories, geographies, and stories of a country's people to make fun and interesting English lessons.

The book grew out of, in large part, a desire to make a reference book for students who attend the myriad English camps held around the world during summers, holidays, and new-year periods. The author, having taught in four such English camps—in his native Vancouver, in Bangkok, in Taipei, and in Shanghai—saw the need for a book specifically created for an English camp. Most English camps are attended by students who possess a wide variety of English-speaking abilities, so this book has three different sections—beginner, intermediate, and advanced—so as to provide material for all levels of students at an English camp.

Each section has fourteen lessons, so there is ample material for an English camp, for students of all levels. Students can work up from one level to the next level, in any particular camp. The advanced students can also work on lower levels if so desired. The main goal of this book is to give students plenty of opportunities to speak. Even though some of the exercises are not specifically speaking lessons, students can pair up after completing a writing or reading lesson, and then practice speaking with the lesson material. Students can also pair up, or form into groups, to discuss the material in any lesson.

This book can also be used as a regular textbook for any ESL (English as a second language) course. Some of the lessons build on one another. Lesson B2—Describing Thai Marine Life—Adjectives, for example, can be used as a prelude to lesson A13—Thai Marine Life—Adjectives, Order of Importance. The book is quite comprehensive in this way.

Teachers will find that there is a lot of material in each lesson, particularly in the advanced sections. In lesson A9—Animism and Rituals in Thai Life—Phrasal Verbs, for example, teachers can make whole lessons just from the vocabulary that is presented in the first part of the lesson. Teachers can then go on and construct a whole lesson from the main exercise, Animism in Thai Life. This also applies to lessons A5, A6, A7, and other lessons in the advanced section.

The introduction to each section presents the necessary grammar for the material in that lesson. The coverage of the grammar is adequate and is not intended to be too rigorous. Practice exercises are always included in each section, giving students ample opportunity to use the material before moving on to the main exercise.

Most texts just focus on one specific language ability or level—beginner, intermediate, or advanced. Students therefore have to purchase a new book once they finish or master a particular level. With *English Camp Thailand,* students have to purchase only one book for all three levels.

B1—Elephants, Whales, and Dolphins

Nouns and Adjectives

A **noun** is a <u>person</u>, <u>place</u>, or <u>thing</u>.

Examples:

Person	Place	Thing
boy	Thailand	pencil
girl	Asia	elephant
teacher	beach	table

An adjective usually <u>describes</u> a <u>noun</u>.

Examples:

Adjective	Noun
pretty	girl
big	elephant
sharp	pencil

There are times when a noun or an adjective can be used to describe the same thing, but in slightly different ways. This is especially true when describing the <u>dimensions</u> of something.

Table 1. Comparing words that express dimensions

Adjectives	Nouns
Long	**Length**
The shark **is** five meters **long**.	The shark **has** a **length** of five meters.
Wide	**Width**
The elephant **was** so **wide** it couldn't fit in the door.	The elephant's **width was** so great it couldn't fit in the door.
High	**Height**
Bangkok's tallest building **is** four hundred meters **high**.	Bangkok's tallest building **has** a **height** of four hundred meters.

1

Deep	Depth
It doesn't matter how **deep** the ocean **is**; a person can still see to the bottom of Kata's beach..	It doesn't matter what the **depth** of the ocean **is**; a person can still see to the bottom of Kata's beach.
Thick	**Thickness**
The dolphin's fin **is** 20 cm **thick**.	The dolphin's fin **has** a **thickness** of 20 cm.

Part 1: Students will learn about the body parts of elephants, whales, and dolphins.

Part 2: Students will measure the lengths of the body parts of elephants, whales, and dolphins. After the body parts have been measured, students will learn how to express these body parts as both nouns and as adjectives. Students then pair up, and with their partner, they can practice speaking by saying the body parts of all the animals shown, as both nouns and adjectives.

Example: Bosley the elephant

Noun: Bosley's tusk **has** a **length** of four units.

In this sentence, the dimensions of Bosley's tusk are expressed as a noun. The dimensions of Bosley's tusk can also be expressed as an adjective.

Adjective: Bosley's tusk **is** four units **long**.

More examples using **nouns** and **adjectives**:

Dolphy the dolphin

Adjective	**Noun**
Dolphy's fin **is** two units **high**.	Dolphy's fin **has** a **height** of two units.
Dolphy's snout **is** two units **long**.	Dolphy's snout **has** a **length** of two units.

Grammar for adjectives: **to be** + measure + **adjective**
    Dolphy's snout **is** two units **long**.

Grammar for nouns: **to be** + **noun** + measure
    Dolphy's snout **has** a **length** of two units.

The Verb **To Be**:

Present   Past
is   was
are   were

Part 1

Do you know the name of an elephant's body parts? Match the words in column A with the words in column B.

Column A

1. _____
2. _____
3. _____
4. _____
5. _____
6. _____
7. _____
8. _____
9. _____
10. _____
11. _____

Column B

a.   baby
b.   chain
c.   ear
d.   eye
e.   mouth
f.   rider (me!)
g.   saddle
h.   tail
i.   toe
j.   trunk
k.   foot

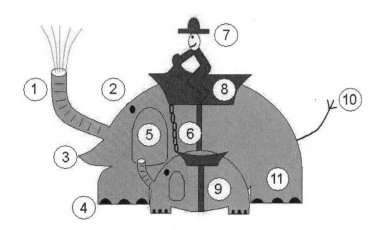

Whales in Thailand

Thai people love whales. Do you know the name of a whale's body parts? Match the words in column A with the words in column B.

Column A

1. _____
2. _____
3. _____
4. _____
5. _____
6. _____
7. _____
8. _____
9. _____

Column B

a. dimple
b. blowhole
c. head
d. eye
e. tummy
f. teeth
g. mouth
h. tail
i. flipper

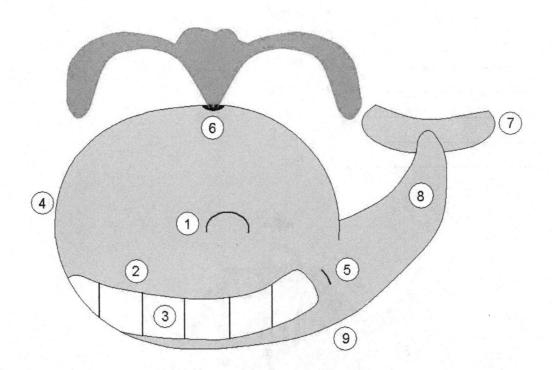

There are a lot of dolphins in Thailand's water. Do you know the name of a dolphin's body parts? Match the words in column A with those in column B.

Column A

1. _____
2. _____
3. _____
4. _____
5. _____
6. _____
7. _____
8. _____

Column B

a. flipper
b. eye
c. body
d. tail
e. tummy
f. snout
g. water
h. fin

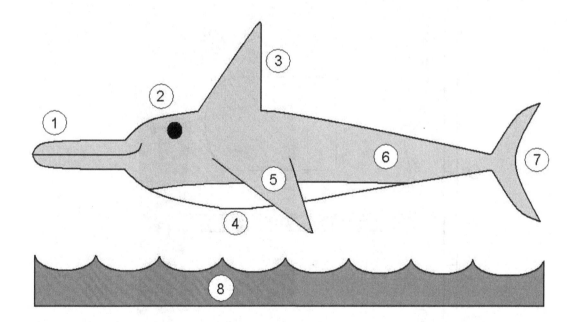

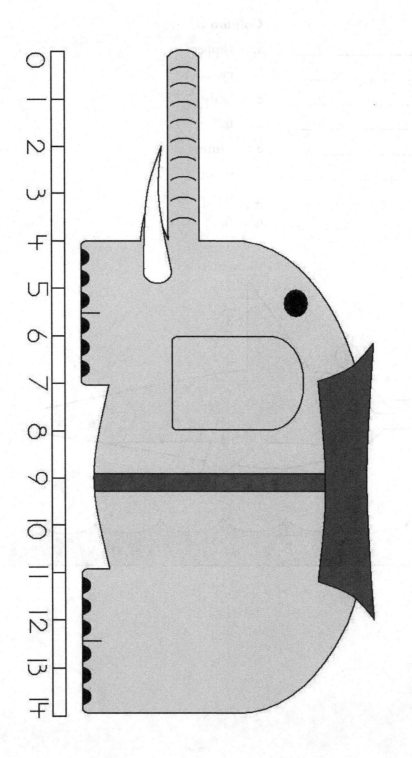

Part 2—Bosley the Elephant

Bosley is a very happy elephant. He loves to play in the water and shoot water out of his trunk. Bosley's friends don't know how long he is or the measurements of his body. Can you help us tell Bosley's friends these things?

1. Bosley's tusk is _____ units long.
2. Bosley's trunk is _____ units long.
3. Bosley's ear is _____ units long.
4. Bosley's saddle is _____ units long.
5. One of Bosley's feet is _____ units long.
6. Two of Bosley's feet are _____ units long.
7. One of Bosley's toenails is _____ units long.
8. Bosley's tummy is _____ units long.
9. Bosley's body is _____ units long.
10. Bosley's trunk is _____ units high.

Part 2—Adjectives and Nouns

Nouns. For nouns, a sentence is said in the following way:

Bosley's <u>ear</u> **has** a **length** of <u>two</u> units.

Adjectives. For adjectives, a sentence is said in the following way:

Bosley's <u>ear</u> **is** <u>two</u> units **long**.

Noun: length   **Adjective:** long

Now practice speaking, using the noun **length** and the adjective **long**.

☐   Student 1:   How **long** is Bosley's _____?
    Student 2:   Bosley's _____ is _____ units **long**.

    Student 1:   What is the **length** of Bosley's _____?
    Student 2:   Bosley's _____ has a **length** of _____ units.

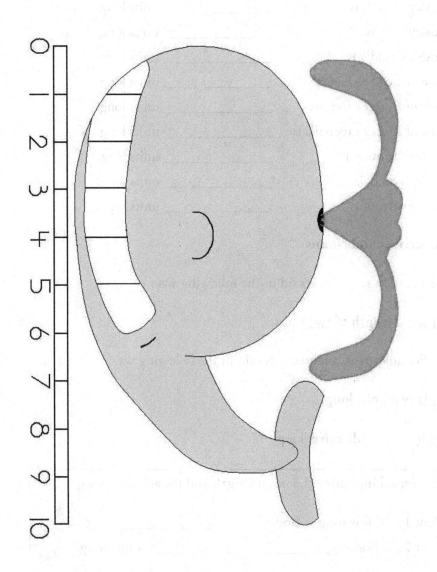

Stumpy the Whale

Stumpy is a very happy whale. Stumpy loves to swim in the ocean and shoot water through her blowhole. Stumpy's friends don't know how long she is or any of the measurements of her body parts. Can you help us tell Stumpy's friends these things?

1. Stumpy's teeth are _____ units long.

2. One tooth is _____ units long.

3. Stumpy's tail is _____ units long.

4. Stumpy's body is _____ units long.

5. Stumpy's head is _____ units long.

6. Stumpy's eye is _____ units long.

7. Stumpy's blowhole is _____ units long.

Noun: length   **Adjective:** long

Now practice speaking, using the noun **length** and the adjective **long**.

Student 1: How **long** is Stumpy's <u>head</u>?

Student 2: Stumpy's <u>head</u> is <u>6.5</u> units **long**.

Student 1: What is the **length** of Stumpy's <u>head</u>?

Student 2: Stumpy's <u>head</u> has a **length** of <u>6.5</u> units.

Use this method to talk about all of Stumpy's body parts.

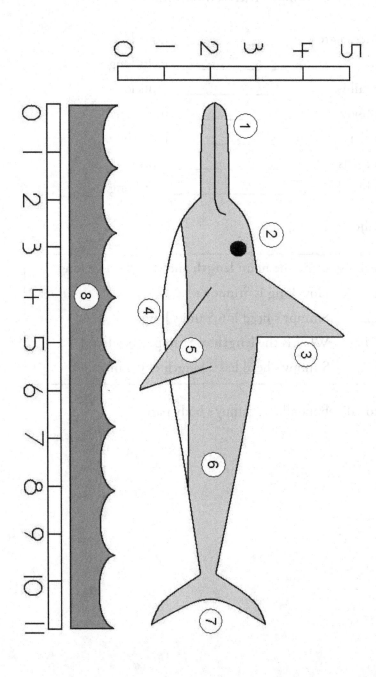

Dolphy the Dolphin

Dolphy is a very happy dolphin. Dolphy loves to swim in the ocean, and she also loves to jump out of the water. Dolphy's friends don't know how long she is or any of the measurements of her body parts. Can you help us tell Dolphy's friends these things?

1. Dolphy's snout is _____ units long.
2. Dolphy's white belly is _____ units long.
3. Dolphy's body is _____ units long.
4. Dolphy's body is _____ units high.
5. Dolphy's tail is _____ units long.
6. Dolphy's tail is _____ units high.
7. Dolphy's fin is _____ units long.
8. Dolphy's fin is _____ units high.
9. Dolphy's flipper is _____ units long.
10. Dolphy's flipper is _____ units high.
11. Dolphy is jumping _____ units high off the water.

Part 2

Noun: length   **Adjective**: long

Now practice speaking, using the noun **length** and the adjective **long**. 　　Student 1:　　How **long** is Dolphy's <u>head</u>? 　　Student 2:　　Dolphy's <u>head is</u> <u>6.5</u> units **long**. 　　Student 1:　　What is the **length** of Dolphy's <u>head</u>? 　　Student 2:　　Dolphy's <u>head</u> has a **length** of <u>6.5</u> units.

B2—Describing Thai Marine Life

Adjectives

An **adjective** is a word that can **describe** a <u>noun</u> or a <u>pronoun</u>.

			Adjective	**Noun**
Whales are	**<u>big</u>**	<u>animals</u>.	**big**	<u>animals</u>
Elephants have	**<u>long</u>**	<u>trunks</u>.	**long**	<u>trunks</u>
Prim likes to drink	**<u>cold</u>**	<u>coconut juice</u>.	**cold**	<u>coconut juice</u>

Adjectives: - qualify nouns and pronouns
   - nearly always appear before a noun or pronoun

Practice Exercises

Place the following **adjectives** in the correct sentences:

<u>beautiful</u>   <u>big</u>   <u>delicious</u>   <u>hot</u>   <u>pointy</u>
<u>clear</u>   sour   <u>tasty</u>   <u>large</u>   <u>striped</u>

1.   Thailand has many   <u>beautiful</u> beaches.
2.   Kanoon's mother makes   _____ pad Thai.
3.   Zebras are   _____ horses.
4.   Grapefruits have a   _____ taste.
5.   The elephant is a   _____ animal.
6.   Thai oceans have   _____ blue water.
7.   Ice cream is a   _____ treat.
8.   Thailand usually has   _____ weather every day.
9.   A Thai wat usually has a   _____ spire on its roof.
10. Bangkok is a very   _____ city.

In the following exercises, use **adjectives** to describe Thai marine life.
There are many beautiful tropical species of marine life in Thai waters. In this lesson, we will make sentences with the following types of marine life:

<u>clownfish</u>   <u>puffer fish</u>   <u>crown of thorns starfish</u>   <u>dugong</u>
<u>scorpion fish</u>   <u>bottlenose dolphin</u>   <u>lagoon triggerfish</u>

Example:

1. (a) The clownfish is a **striped** fish.
         The **stripes** of the clownfish are **black**.
    (b) The clownfish has an **orange** face.

Now write a few of your own sentences about the **clownfish**:

(c) _____

(d) _____

(e) _____

This table of adjectives will help you describe Thai marine life:

Determiner	Size and Shape	Observation	Color/Appearance
a	big	beautiful	blue
an	huge	pretty	red
for	large	gorgeous	orange
the	sizeable	good-looking	yellow
	small	handsome	purple
	tiny	ravishing	striped
	little	shiny	brightly colored
	round	ugly	dull
	oblong	horrid	bright
	square	hideous	silvery
	oval	unsightly	golden

The Puffer Fish

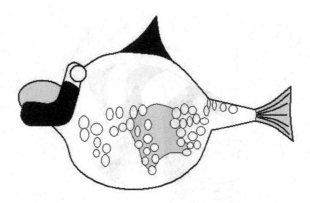

1. (a) The puffer fish has a **big, round** belly when it puffs itself up.

   (b) The puffer fish has a **round** belly.

   (c) _____

   (d) _____

   (e) _____

The Crown of Thorns Starfish

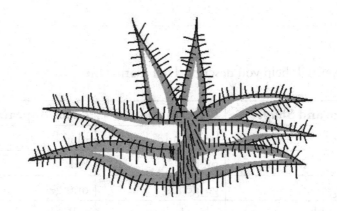

2. (a) _____

   (b) _____

   (c) _____

   (d) _____

   (e) _____

The Dugong

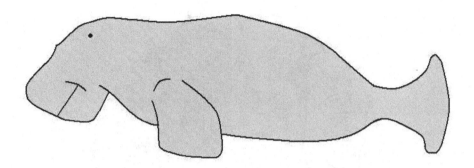

3. (a) _____
    (b) _____
    (c) _____
    (d) _____
    (e) _____

Bottlenose Dolphin

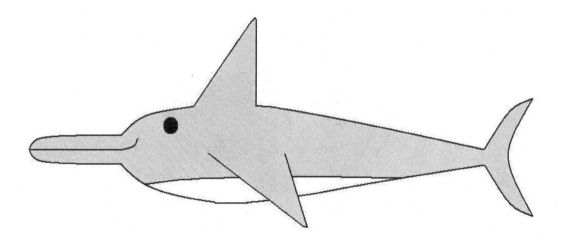

4. (a) _____
    (b) _____
    (c) _____
    (d) _____
    (e) _____

Scorpion Fish

5. (a) _____

   (b) _____

   (c) _____

   (d) _____

   (e) _____

The Cuttlefish

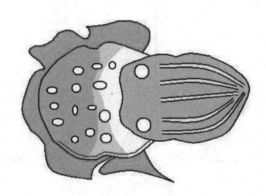

6. (a) _____

   (b) _____

   (c) _____

   (d) _____

   (e) _____

The Lagoon Triggerfish

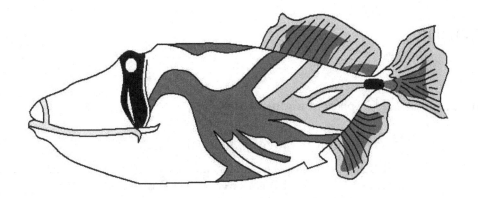

7. (a) _____

    (b) _____

    (c) _____

    (d) _____

    (e) _____

B3—Thai Kids

Pronouns

Pronouns are often used in place of **nouns** in sentences.

The following table shows the different kinds of pronouns:

Subject Pronouns	Object Pronouns	Possessive Adjectives	Possessive Pronouns
The subjects of a sentence	The objects of a sentence		Shows ownership. They are not followed by a noun.
I	me	my	mine
he	him	his	his
she	her	her	hers
it	it	its	
we	us	our	ours
you	you	your	yours
they	them	their	theirs

Grammar Note: Learn this grammar because you will be using it later.

The **subject** of a **verb** is the <u>person</u> or <u>thing</u> that **performs** an <u>action</u>.

The **object** of a **verb** is the <u>person</u> or <u>thing</u> that **receives** an <u>action</u>.

<u>Subject</u>	<u>Verb</u>	<u>Object</u>
I	like	her.

I **performs** the action.
Her **receives** the action.

<u>Subject</u>	<u>Verb</u>	<u>Object</u>
That book	is	mine.

That book **performs** the action.
Mine **receives** the action.

18

The following **pronouns** are **singular:**

I	me	mine	she	her	hers	he	him	you	yours	it	its

The following **pronouns** are **plural:**

we	us	ours	you	yours	they	theirs

A **pronoun** must agree in (a) gender (male or female)
(b) number (singular or plural)
with the **word (noun)** it is replacing.

Examples: Peera **is** a boy. He **is** five years old.
          Peera and Tul **are** boys. They **are** five years old.

(1)   Peera is a **boy**, so the **pronoun** must be **male**.   (a) gender
       Peera is a **singular noun** so the **pronoun** must be **singular**.
                                                            (b) number

(2)   Peera and Tul are **boys**, so the **pronoun** must be **male**.
                                                            (a) gender
       There is **more than one** boy, so the **pronoun** must be **plural**.
                                                            (b) number

Sample Sentences

   1. Tim didn't study much, so I think **he** won't do well on his test.

   2. Pop gave me the ball. **She** didn't want to play with **it** anymore.

   3. Kanoon slept in today. **Her** alarm clock didn't ring.

Practice Exercises. Choose the correct **pronoun** in the sentences.

   1. Whose book is this? It is **(I / mine)** <u>mine</u>.

   2. Prang is a wonderful person; **(her / she's)** _____ my best friend.

   3. The red book belongs to **(me / mine)** _____, and I think the blue
       book belongs to **(you / yours)** _____.

4. The red book is (**me / mine**) _____, and I think the blue book is (**you / yours**) _____.

5. Suchera always wears nice clothes. I think (**her / hers**) _____ mother and father own a clothing store.

6. The boys are playing basketball now, but (**they / their**) _____will finish playing soon.

7. (**We / Us**) _____ should go watch that new movie tonight.

8. My dad and (**I / they**) _____ will celebrate (**my / I**) _____ birthday tomorrow.

9. (**We / Our**) _____ should have lunch now. It's past noon.

10. Prim is (**my / mine**) _____ best friend, but I think everyone else also likes (**she / her**) _____ very much.

Main Exercise: Singular and Plural Pronouns

Put the following **pronouns** into the sentences below:

Singular Pronouns

I	me	she	her	he	his	my

Plural Pronouns

we	us	our	they

1. (a)   <u>His</u> name is Peera. <u>He</u> is a boy.

   (b)   <u>My</u> name is Peera. <u>I</u> am a boy.

2. Jan and Jen are sisters. _____ are twins. _____ both have black hair.

3. _____ am Poon. _____ is Sanuk. _____ are friends.

4. Jambon is a man. _____ is my teacher. _____ am Pun.

 _____ am Jambon's student.

5. Who am _____? _____ am Khae. _____ am five years old.

6. Who is _____? _____ is Top. _____ are friends.

 _____ are also classmates.

7. Who are _____? _____ are my three new friends. _____ are the new students.

8. Who is _____? _____ name is May. _____ is a girl.

9. _____ am Look Mee. _____ is Pol. _____ is my dad.

 _____ is a fireman.

10. _____ am Peter. _____ is Bob. _____ are friends.

11. _____ name is Meena. _____ mother is a doctor.

 _____ works in a hospital.

12. _____ dog is cute. _____ name is Fido. _____ is a poodle.

 _____ parents are cool. _____ mom's name is Krit. _____ is

13. beautiful. _____ dad's name is Song. _____ is handsome.

B4—Popeye, Baby, and Jumpy

Comparatives and Superlatives

(1)   **Comparatives**—used when comparing two things

(a)   Examples of comparatives:

Regular Word	Comparative
big	bigger
long	longer
funny	funnier

Examples: The elephant is **bigger** than the monkey.

                 The girl clown is **funnier** than the boy clown.

                 Jane's car is **faster** than my car.

(b)   Comparatives with only one or two syllables

The following comparatives have two syllables:

Word	**Syllables**	
bigger	big	ger
longer	lon	ger

– For most of these types of comparatives, just add **er** to the end of the word.

– For some comparatives, like **big**, you may have to add an <u>additional letter</u>, like **g**, to the word before adding **er**.

– For most words that end in **y**, like **funny**, change the **y** to **i** before adding **er**.

(c)   Comparatives with three or more syllables

When making comparisons between words with **three or more syllables** (beau / ti / ful has three syllables), use the word **more** when **comparing two things**.

Examples:

Regular Word	Comparative
beautiful	more beautiful
enchanting	more enchanting

The lady in the evening gown is **more beautiful** than the lady with the skirt.

Word	Syllables
beautiful	beau / ti / ful
enchanting	en / chan / ting

(2) **Superlatives**—used when comparing three or more things

(a) Examples of superlatives:

Regular Word	Superlative
big	biggest
long	longest
funny	funniest

Examples: Tom is the **tallest** person in our school.

Russia is the **biggest** country in the world.

(b) Superlatives with one or two syllables.

– For most of these types of superlatives, just add **est** to the end of the word.
– For some superlatives, like **big**, you may have to add an <u>additional letter</u>, like **g**, to the word before adding **est**.
– When a word ends in **y**, like **funny**, change the **y** to **i** before adding **est**.

(c) Superlatives with three or more syllables

When comparing words with **three or more syllables** (beau /ti /ful has three syllables), use the words **the most** when **comparing three or more things**.

Word	Syllables
beautiful	beau / ti / ful
enchanting	en / chan / ting

Examples:

Regular Word	Superlative
beautiful	the most beautiful
enchanting	the most enchanting
entertaining	the most entertaining

Example: Last night's concert was the **most entertaining** concert I have ever been to.

(3)   Summary

Regular Word	Comparative	Superlative
small	smaller	smallest
bright	brighter	brightest
shiny	shinier	shiniest
beautiful	more beautiful	the most beautiful
interesting	more interesting	the most interesting

Practice Exercises. In the sentences below, **circle** the correct word/s.

1. Elephants are among the **bigger / biggest** animals in the world.

2. A car is **more expensive / most expensive** to own than a bicycle.

3. Santul is **taller / tallest** than his younger brother.

4. The **higher / highest** mountain in the USA is in Alaska.

5. Thailand is the **more popular / most popular** country to visit in Southeast Asia.

6. Bangkok is Thailand's **bigger / biggest** and **busier / busiest** city.

7. African elephants are **bigger / biggest** than Asian elephants.

8. The **finer / finest** beaches in Thailand are located in Krabi.

9. The summer of 2015 was **hotter / the hottest** summer ever in Canada.

10. The **higher / highest** mountains in Thailand are in the north.

11. Southern Thailand has the **more diverse / most diverse** rainforests in the country.

12. The Carmanah Giant on Vancouver Island, which is over ninety-five meters high, is the world's **larger / largest** Sitka spruce tree.

13. The Loi Krathong festival, where people place flowers and incense on boats in the river, is **more enchanting / the most enchanting** festival in Thailand.

14. The Great Chedi of Nakoh Pathon is the **taller / tallest** Buddha monument in the world. It is 127 meters high.

15. Soccer is the **more popular / most popular** sport in the world. In America, American football is **more popular / the most popular**.

16. Thai food is amongst the **spicier / spiciest** food in the world.

17. The **earlier / earliest** capital in Thailand was Sukhotha. It was founded in the thirteenth century.

18. Riding elephants is one of the **more fun / most fun** things to do in Thailand.

19. The **noisier / noisiest** time of day in a Thai rain forest is the morning, after the birds, monkeys and frogs wake up, and start to call out to each other.

20. The **more brilliant / most brilliant** fish in the world are in Thai waters.

Main Exercise: Use either the **comparative** or the **superlative** when comparing elephants or other animals listed below.

Popeye   Baby   Jumpy

1. Baby is **(small)** ___smaller___ than Jumpy.

2. Elephants are the **(big)** _____ animals in the world.

3. Popeye is playing with the **(small)** _____ ball.

4. Elephants are the **(enchanting)** _____ animals in the world.

5. Baby is playing with the **(interesting)** _____ ball.

6. The yellow ball is **(big)** _____ than the blue ball.

7. Popeye has the **(big)** _____ eyes.

8. Baby's ball is the **(colorful)** _____.

9. Popeye's trunk reaches the **(high)** _____.

10. Baby's toes are the **(small)** _____.

11. A monkey is much **(small)** _____ than an elephant.

12. Popeye has the **(big)** _____ trunk.

13. Baby's ear is **(small)** _____ than Popeye's.

14. Elephants are amongst **(intelligent)** _____ and **(good-natured)** _____ animals in the world.

15. Baby's trunk is **(small)** _____ than Jumpy's.

16. Elephants can shoot **(powerful)** _____ jet stream of water out of their trunks.

17. Elephant have (big) _____ feet than hippos.

18. Popeye can shoot a (powerful) _____ jet stream of water out of his trunk than Baby.

19. Jumpy's toes are (small) _____ than Popeye's toes.

20. Popeye can carry (heavy) _____ people.

21. A giraffe can reach (high) _____ than an elephant.

22. Baby is fitted with the (small) _____ saddle.

23. African elephants are (big) _____ and (heavy) _____ than Asian elephants.

24. Riding an elephant can be (extraordinary) _____ experience a person can have.

25. Riding an elephant can also be (dangerous) _____ experience for a person if the elephant starts to stampede.

26. Baby's stomach is (low) _____ to the ground than is Jumpy's.

27. The elephant can be amongst (immovable) _____ animals because of their great weight.

28. Elephants' trunks are (flexible) _____ than their tusks.

29. Elephants' tusks are (pointy) _____ than their trunks.

30. Baby has the (short) _____ trunk.

31. Elephants are (heavy) _____ than giraffes.

32. An elephant can run (fast) _____ than a turtle.

B5—Thai Marine Life

Plural and Singular Nouns
Regular and Irregular Nouns

Plural nouns can be regular or irregular.

Regular Nouns

(i) For regular nouns, form the **plural** by **adding s** to the end of the word.

(ii) If the **singular noun** ends in **y**, like **party**, then form the **plural** by **changing** the **y** to **i** and then adding **es** to the end of the word. For some singular nouns that end with **y**, just add **s** to the end of the noun.

(iii) If a noun ends in **ch**, like **beach**, form the **plural** by **adding es** to the end.

Type	Noun Ending	Singular Noun	Plural
(i)	Regular noun	girl	girls
(ii)	y	party	parties
(ii)	At times, when the noun ends in "y," just add "s" to the end of the noun	monkey	monkeys
(iii)	ch	beach	beaches

Irregular Nouns

It is not easy to know how to form a plural for an irregular noun. Irregular nouns like <u>fish</u>, <u>sheep</u>, and <u>shrimp</u> are the same for the singular and plural. For other irregular nouns, there are no set rules for forming the plural.

Examples: Plurals of regular and irregular nouns used in this lesson:

Noun	Regular Plural	Irregular Plural
algae		algae
arm	arms	
beach	beaches	
belly	bellies	
blood		blood

body	bodies	
clownfish		clownfish
coral reef	coral reefs	
dolphin	dolphins	
drink	drinks	
dugong	dugongs	
eye	eyes	
fin	fins	
fish		fish
flipper	flippers	
foot		feet
gill	gills	
leaf		leaves
leg	legs	
life		lives
man		men
mermaid	mermaids	
merman		mermen
neck	necks	
octopus		octopi
predator	predators	
sand	sands	sand
school	schools	
shark	sharks	
sheep		sheep
shell	shells	
shelf		shelves
shrimp		shrimp
snout	snouts	
stripe	stripes	
swordfish		swordfish
tail	tails	
tear	tears	
tooth		teeth
turtle	turtles	
water	waters	water
wave	waves	
woman		women

Practice: Write the plural form of the singular noun for each sentence.

1. The shark broke <u>one</u>   **tooth**.   **Tooth** is a **singular** noun.
   The shark broke <u>many</u>   **teeth**.   **Teeth** is a **plural** noun.

2. One **turtle** was swimming.   (singular)
   Five _____ were swimming.   (plural)

3. My right **foot** is sore.
   Mermaid do not have any _____.

4. A dugong has a **tail**.
   Many species of fish have _____.

5. I only ate one **shrimp** at lunch.
   Toon ate many _____ at lunch.

6. Ko Samui has a beautiful **beach**.
   Thailand has many beautiful _____.

7. Prim's **eye** got water in it.
   Both of Prim's _____ got water in them.

8. One **fish** swam by our boat.
   Many _____ swam by our boat.

9. Prang cut her **toe** on a rock.
   Bumbimh has many _____.

10. Krit was surfing on a **wave**.
    I wanted to surf today, but there weren't any high _____ in the ocean.

11. I got a grain of **sand** in my shoe.
    There is a lot of _____ on the beach.

12. Kanoon drank a coconut **drink**.
    We drank many coconut _____.

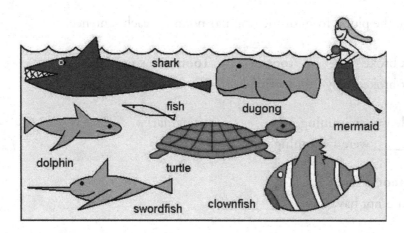

Change the nouns to their **plural** form. Refer to the picture above.

1. The **(tooth)** _____ of the shark are razor sharp.

2. The **(snout)** _____ of swordfish are pointy.

3. There are many kinds of **(fish)** _____ in Thailand.

4. Fish don't have a **(foot)**.   Fish don't have _____.

5. Fish also don't have an **(arm)**.   Fish also don't have _____.

6. Fish also don't have a **(neck)**.   Fish also don't have _____.

7. Most fish breathe through their **(gill)** _____.

8. The **(shell)** _____ of turtles have many different colors.

9. Mermaids can be classified as being **(woman)** _____.

10. The octopus has eight **(arm)** _____.

11. Groups of fish travel together in **(school)** _____.

12. There are many **(predator)** _____ in Thai waters, like sharks.

13. The two **(octopus)** _____ fed on the dead shark.

14. Turtles hide in their **(shell)** _____ when they are frightened.

15. Many fish swim close to the **(shelf)** _____ of ocean floors.

16. Some fish rub their **(belly)** _____ on the ocean floor.

17. The clownfish hides in **(coral reef)** _____.

18. There are many different types of **(algae)** _____ in the ocean.

19. There are many **shrimp** _____ in the ocean for fish to eat.

20. The **(beach)** _____ of Thailand are full of fish.

21. Loi Krathong, a festival in Thailand, is held in order to make sure that the **(water)** _____ in Thailand recede.

22. Dugong's **(tear)** _____ are collected and then made into charms.

23. The **(life)** _____ of many different types of marine life can be easily ended if they are eaten by other types of marine life.

24. Fish can lose a lot of **(blood)** _____ if they accidentally scrape themselves against the sharp coral of the coral reefs.

25. The **(leaf)** _____ of underwater plants can provide cover for fish if they are being pursued by predators.

26. Clownfish have many **(stripe)** _____ on their bodies.

B6—Thai Marine Life

Prepositions

There are many different types of marine life in Thai waters, like the dugong (often nicknamed the sea cow), sharks, and turtles.

The following species can be found in Thai waters:

Shark
Tiger sharks are commonly found in Thai waters.

Dugong
The dugong is related to the elephant. Dugongs graze on underwater grasses during the day and night, and they can stay beneath the surface for six minutes without coming up for air.

Fish
Thai waters have more than eight hundred kinds of open-water fish and more than three hundred types of fish that live on the ocean floor.

Dolphin
The bottlenose dolphin is the main type of dolphin in Thailand.

Turtle
There are four main types of turtles in Thai waters. The most common turtle is the leatherback turtle.

Clownfish
The clownfish usually swims around coral reefs. It uses its bright colors to camouflage itself, so as to avoid predators.

Swordfish
The swordfish swims in the open seas. The bones of its upper jaw are arranged so that they form the shape of a sword.

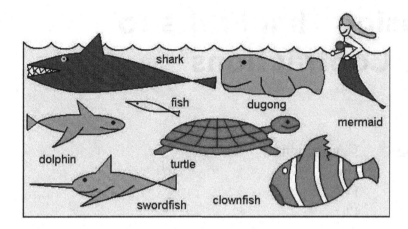

Practice Exercise: Use the **prepositions** below to describe the positions of marine life in the picture above.

above	behind	below	from	front	in between
next to	on	out of	on top of	under	close to

Example: The shark is **on top of / above** the dolphin.
The shark is **above** the swordfish.
The shark is **next to** the dugong.
The shark's fin is **out of** the water.

Do the exercises in appendix B before doing this main exercise.

Main Exercise: Make sentences using the **prepositions** above.

1. <u>fish</u>   The fish is   **<u>under</u>**   the shark.

2. <u>dugong</u>

3. <u>mermaid</u>

4. <u>dolphin</u>

5. <u>turtle</u>

6. <u>swordfish</u>

7. <u>clownfish</u>

B7—Using Thai Fruits to Study Contractions

Regular Words	Contractions
I am	I'm
I have	I've
I will	I'll
he is	he's
he is not	he isn't
	he's not
she is	she's
she is not	she isn't
	she's not
it is	it's
it is not	it isn't
	it's not
we are	we're
we have	we've
we will	we'll
we will not	we won't
they are	they're
they are not	they're not
	they aren't
they have	they've

Rules for Using Contractions

1. When <u>speaking</u> or using <u>informal writing</u> in the English language, we often use contractions (or short forms).

    Instead of saying **I am,** **she is,** and **we are**
    we say **I'm,** **she's,** and **we're.**

34

In <u>formal writing</u>, we usually use the full words, *not* the contraction.

Instead of writing   **I'm**,   **she's,** and   **we're**
    we write   **I am**,   **she is,** and   **we are**.

2. Do **not** use **'m, 's, 'd, 're,** or **'ll** at the end of a sentence.

3. For these types of sentences, the <u>long form</u> **must** be used.

	<u>Correct</u>	<u>Incorrect</u>
Are you hungry?	Yes **<u>I am</u>**.	Yes **<u>I'm</u>**.
	I know where **<u>he is</u>**.	I know where **<u>he's</u>**.

4. Some <u>short forms</u> will be the **same**, but the <u>long forms</u> can be **different**. You must therefore watch out for this and recognize it.

<u>He has</u> gone away. **<u>He's</u>** gone away.
<u>He is</u> sick now. **<u>He's</u>** sick now.

<u>He's</u> means something different in each sentence. When reading English, you must be sure to examine the whole sentence in order to make sure that you understand the contraction properly.

Practice Exercises: Place the correct **contraction** in the blank.

1. (**I'm / I'll**) _____ with my parents tonight.

2. (**I'm / I'll**) _____ be with my parents tonight.

3. (**They've / They'll**) _____ been dating for one year.

4. Prang is the nicest girl in our school. (**She's / He's**) _____ always very polite and courteous.

5. The students have been working hard, but I don't think (**they'll / they've**) _____ finish chapter 2 by today.

6. Ming is very tidy. (**She's / I'm**) _____ so neat.

7. Jobim has a cold today. (**He's / They're**) _____ quite sick.

8. (**Jobim's / Jobim'll**) _____ got a cold today.

9. (**Jobim's / Jobim'll**) _____ get a cold if he doesn't wear a jacket.

10. Kong is an intelligent boy, but (**he's / she's**) _____ still not getting A's in every subject.

11. Everyone is going to the park, but **(we'll / we're)** _____ have to bring our lunch, because there is no food for sale there.

12. Where are Mint and Kanoon? **(They're / They've)** _____ in the park now, but they should be home soon.

13. Where are Mint and Kanoon? **(They're / They've)** _____ been playing volleyball in the park, but they should be home soon.

Thai Fruits

The following fruits are very popular in Thailand.

banana
coconut
dragonfruit
durian
jackfruit
langsat
longon
lychee
mafai
mango
mangosteen
papaya
pineapple
pomelo
rambutan
roseapple
sala
santol
snakefruit
tamarind

Main Exercise: Choose the correct **contraction** from the choices given.

1. My friends told me to try to eat durian, but **(I'm / I'll)** _____ afraid to because it has a strong taste.
2. Bom Bim is a wonderful person. **(She's / We're)** _____ my best friend, but I still didn't eat durian when she offered me some.

3. Bom Bim is a wonderful person. **(She's / we're)** _____ best friends, but I still didn't eat durian when she offered me some.
4. **(I've / I'm)** _____ got some jackfruit at home, so let's go make a drink of halo halo.
5. **(We're / We'll)** _____ going to climb a banana tree to get some bananas. Peera **(isn't / he's not)** _____ coming though.
6. **(We're / we'll)** _____ climb banana trees this afternoon to get some bananas. Peera **(isn't / won't)** _____ be coming though.
7. **(We're / We'll)** _____ climb banana trees this afternoon to get some bananas. Peera **(won't / isn't)** _____ coming though.
8. **(It's / We're)** _____ too hot to swim at the beach. Let's have a coconut drink under the trees instead.
9. Is Krit coming with us to the store? Yes, **(she is / she's)** _____.
10. Tata Young is having a concert tonight. **(Let's / We're)** _____ go have a pineapple drink before we go watch the concert.
11. Have you eaten mangos and papayas before? **(They're / They've)** _____ delicious.
12. Have you eaten mangos and papayas before? **(They're / They've)** _____ got a delicious taste.
13. The Thais have written a song about the longon because **(it's / it's not)** _____ such a popular fruit. They really love to eat it.
14. The lychee is popular not only in Thailand but in the rest of the world as well. **(They're / They're not)** _____ so delicious.
15. The snake fruit has a strange flavor. **(It's / They're)** _____ both smoky and tangy.
16. The snake **(fruit's / fruit it's)** _____ got a juicy taste, but the fruit is quite firm. **(It's / They've)** _____ got a large stone inside, so there **(isn't / it's)** _____ much fruit inside it.
17. Pomelos are similar to grapefruits, but **(aren't / isn't)** _____ as sour.
18. The pomelo is similar to the grapefruit, but **(aren't / isn't)** _____ as sour.
19. The langsat has a sweet taste, but it's very sticky, so **(we'll / we've)** _____ have to wash our hands after eating them.
20. The langsat has a sweet taste, but it's very sticky, so **(we'll / we've)** _____ got to wash our hands after eating them.
21. The rambutan has a stone inside it. **(It's / They're)** _____ in the center of the fruit.
22. Rambutans have stones inside them. **(It's / They're)** _____ in the center of the fruit.

23. The tamarind is sweet inside, and it has the texture of a raisin. **(It's / They're)** _____ my favorite fruit.

24. The mangosteen is often called the queen of Thai fruits. **(It's / She's)** _____ delicious and sweet.

25. Do you like rose apples better, or do you prefer the sala? **(I've / I'm)** _____ tried both of them, and I prefer rose apples.

B8—Recycling and the Environment

Antonyms and Synonyms

Synonyms: words that have the **same** or **similar** meanings.
Antonyms: words that have **opposite** meanings.

Bosley is a **big** elephant.	Bosley is a **large** elephant.
The word **large** is a **synonym** of the word **big**.	

Bosley is a **big** elephant.	Popeye is a **small** elephant.
The word **small** is an **antonym** of the word **big**.	

Example: **synonyms** and **antonyms** using the word **big**

Word	Synonym	Antonym
big	large	small
	huge	tiny
	humungous	little
	immense	wee
	massive	petite

Practice Exercise: Write **two synonyms** and **two antonyms** for each word.

Word	Synonym	Antonym
over	above on top of	under below
old	aged	young
hot		
pretty	beautiful	
far		
messy		
wet	moist	
high		low
long		short
messy	dirty	

39

Practice: Circle the **synonym** that matches the given word. Refer to the picture.

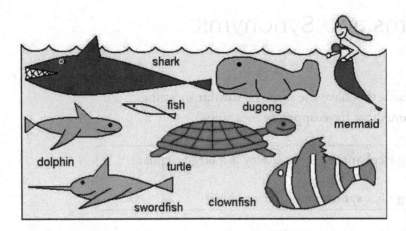

1. Kanoon is very **pretty (beautiful / plain looking)**.
2. The dolphin swam **quickly (slowly / rapidly)** through the waters.
3. Pad Thai is very **delicious (awful / tasty)**.
4. It is **dangerous (safe / unsafe)** to get too close to a shark.
5. The beach is **close (near / far)** to the hotel.
6. Phuket has the **most (least / greatest number of)** beaches in Thailand.
7. My mother cooks the **tastiest (most delicious / blandest)** Thom Yan.
8. My surfboard is **under (on top of / below)** the table.
9. Hua Hin is **near (close to / far from)** Bangkok.
10. The clownfish has **many (few / lots of)** stripes.
11. The head of the dugong is quite **round (flat / curved)**.
12. The nose of the swordfish is very **sharp (pointy / dull)**.
13. Coconut juice is very **sweet (bitter / sugary)**.
14. The water at Krabi is very, very **clear (murky / transparent)**.
15. The legend of the mermaid is **imaginary (true / not true)**.
16. We saw a **gigantic (huge / tiny)** shark at Kata Beach today.
17. African elephants are **bigger (larger / smaller)** than Asian elephants.
18. The green shell of the turtle is **hard (soft / tough)**.
19. We ate octopus on the stick at Hua Hin, and it was **spicy (mild / hot)**.
20. It was too **hot (warm / cold)** to be in the sun for too long today.

Note: **Hot** can refer to temperature, but it can also describe food and whether the food is spicy or mild tasting.

Important Words. The following words are used in the story. Most of the words are quite easy. Read them over and make sure you understand them.

Nouns

air conditioner	- a machine that is used in a closed room to make the air cooler and to make the temperature lower
coral reef	- rocks at the bottom of the sea, formed when skeletons of dead marine life fall to the bottom of the sea
danger	- to be exposed to injury, loss, evil, or peril
eco-shower	- a type of shower where people try to use less water
environment	- often refers to the earth's environment, which is its land, sea, and air
fan	- a machine that makes air move so that the air is cooler
marine life	- all the different types of fish in the ocean or the sea
noise	- loud or disturbing sounds
petrol	- gasoline
plant life	- plants or trees
pollution	- air, water, or soil that has been made dirty or unclean
refuse	- garbage
responsibility	- duty
	- an ability to meet an obligation
safety	- to be away from danger, injury, or risk
threat	- a sign of coming danger, injury, or risk
tourist	- a visitor to another country

Adjectives

horrible	- bad, terrible, the worst thing
polluted	- something that is dirty or unclean

Verbs

confuse	- to mix up
	- to mix up someone or something mentally
conserve	- to maintain, to protect, to preserve
	- to keep from being lost
	- to keep from being thrown away or wasted
pollute	- to make something dirty or unclean
popular	- well liked
	- admired
protect	- to defend
	- to make something safe or safer
prevent	- to stop something from happening
reuse / recycle	- to use again

(Note to Teacher: It is possible to make a whole lesson with the words above.)

Story 1—Kids and the Environment: Saving Thailand's Oceans

Choose the correct **synonym** in the parentheses.

1. Kids have a very **special (important / small)** responsibility: they must protect the environment. Earth is becoming more polluted, and many animals, fish, and plants are dying because of what human beings are doing to the earth. **Many (fewer / lots of)** people go to Thailand's beaches, so this can be **bad (terrible / good)** for the animals, plant life, and fish there. Kids can help governments make rules to protect Thai beaches.

2. Thailand has over eight hundred **kinds (types / shells)** of open-water **fish (marine life / farm animals)** and three hundred types that **live (dwell / die)** on the **floor (bottom / top)** of the sea. If people catch and eat too many fish, there will be less and less fish in the sea. This is not the only **threat (danger / safety)** to fish, though. More **tourists (visitors / local people)** are coming to Thailand, and when tourists use boats, these boats can hit marine life under the sea and kill them.

3. Many dugong die each year because dugongs swim **close to (near to / far from)** the surface, and boats often **hit (run into / miss)** them. Powerboats also use **gas (petrol / electricity),** so they pollute the water fish swim in. The boats also make too much noise, and this **disturbs (confuses / gladdens)** the fish under the water.

4. Coral gardens (coral reefs) under the sea are also being **destroyed (ruined / made)**. A coral garden can support **over (more than / less than)** one hundred **types (species / fins)** of marine life. Pollution can kill the coral, so this destroys the place where fish live. Marine life, like the clownfish, polka-dotted grunts, sea fans, and barrel sponges swim **among (around / outside)** the reefs, and pollution kills coral reefs and marine life living there.

5. The beaches' plant life is also being destroyed. Many people go to the Kopangang Moon Festival, but trees are **cut down (chopped down / (planted)** to make room for people. **Trees (plant life / fish)** are destroyed when too many people **crowd (gather at / stay away from)** the beach and then **walk on (step on / avoid)** the plants. One of the **worst (very bad / best)** things is when people throw **garbage (refuse / treasure)** in the sea or on the beach. Thai kids want to use their **beautiful (gorgeous / simple)** beaches when they grow up, so it is up to them to protect their beaches.

Postreading Exercise: Which paragraph (1–5) contains the following information? Paragraph 5 can be used more than once.

   1. People throw too much garbage on the beach. _____
   2. Marine life can be killed if it is hit by boats. _____
   3. Thai kids have a responsibility to protect their beaches. _____
   4. Too many people on the beach can destroy plant life. _____
   5. Thailand has over one thousand types of marine life in its waters. _____
   6. Different types of fish live in the coral gardens. _____

Story 2—Recycling, Reusing, and Saving Power

Using Less Water

6.   Even though Thai kids can help save their beaches from pollution, there are other things they can do at home to protect planet Earth. Taking a shower can use eleven liters of water each minute, so it is **better (worse / advantageous)** to take **shorter (longer / quicker)** showers. Kids can also take eco-showers. To do this, kids first get wet and then turn the water off. Then you can soap and shampoo yourself when the water is off. When you are finished soaping yourself, turn the water back on to wash off the soap and shampoo. Kids can also tell their parents to **reuse (recycle / waste)** water. When parents wash vegetables or fruits, kids can tell them to save this water and use it to water the plants outside the house.

Saving Electricity and Power

7.   It can also be easy to use less power. Nearly everyone owns a computer, but laptops use less **power (energy / gas)** than desktop computers. Desktops can use up to five times more power than a laptop. Kids can also tell everyone to **turn the lights off (turn the lights on / close the lights)** when they are not being used. Fans also use a lot less energy than air conditioners do, so it is better to use a fan. Kids can also tell their parents to walk or use a bicycle instead of **driving (operating / buying)** a car.

Recycle

8.   Kids can also tell parents to **recycle (ride a bicycle / reuse things)**. If parents **buy (purchase / sell)** recycled products, this will conserve energy and materials. Kids can also make sure they put all used plastics and bottles into the recycle bin. Clothes, furniture, and many other things can be **made (produced / thrown away)** from recycled products. People can reuse what they have instead of **throwing it away (discarding it / keeping it)**. There are many things Thai kids can do to help save the environment.

Postreading Exercise: Which paragraph (6–8) contains the following information?

1.   Eco-showers are fun, and they can save water.   _____
2.   Recycling used things is a great way to conserve energy.   _____
3.   Laptop computers use less energy than desktop computers.   _____

B9—Describing Thai People

Inversion and Do
Changing Sentences into Questions

In this lesson, you will learn two ways to change declarative sentences into sentences that **ask questions**, using (A) **inversion** (B) the word **do.**

(A) Inversion, Invert: To turn something over; or to turn something upside down.

In English grammar, inversion means to **reverse** the usual order of words, in order to make a question.

Examples: Making a **question** out of a sentence that contains the verb "**be**"

Subject	Verb	Sentence	Question
you	are	**You are** a boy.	**Are you** a boy?
she	is	**She is** fine.	**Is she** fine?
they	are	**They are** Thai.	**Are they** Thai?

Simply invert the position of the subject and the verb to make a question.

Grammar:	Original sentence:	**Subject**	**Verb**	**Object**
	Question:	**Verb**	**Subject**	**Object**

(B) Making Questions out of Sentences with "Do"

Questions can also be made from sentences with the verb "**do.**" To make a question, simply put the verb "**do**" in front of the original sentence.

Subject	Verb	Original Sentence	Question
Mook	hates	**Mook hates** rain.	<u>**Does** Mook hate</u> rain?
Chaiyo	likes	**Chaiyo likes** apples.	<u>**Does** Chaiyo like</u> apples?
She	studied	**She studied** hard.	<u>**Did** she study</u> hard?

Grammar:	Original sentence:		**Subject**	**Verb**	**Object**
	Question:	**Do / Does**	**Subject**	**Verb**	**Object**

Note: If the verb is in the present tense in the original sentence, the verb changes into the past tense in the question (and vice versa). **Do** is then formed in the past tense in the question (and vice versa).

For the sentence: **She studied hard.**

In the original sentence, **study** is in the **past tense.**
So in the question, **study** is **changed** into the **present tense.**

Do:

Present tense: do
Past tense: did, does

Practice: Change the sentences into questions or change the question into sentences.

A—The Verb "To Be"

1. (a) <u>Mike</u> **is** a boy.
    (b) **Is** <u>Mike</u> a boy?

2. (a) <u>Kikkik</u> **is** going home at 5:00 p.m.
    (b) _____

3. (a) _____
    (b) **Are** <u>Suchera and Cham Chon</u> from Bangkok?

4. (a) We **<u>were</u>** going to the park.
    (b) _____

5. (a) _____
    (b) **Were** <u>they</u> at the party?

6. (a) **Am** <u>I</u> allowed to go fishing?
    (b) _____

7. (a) _____
    (b) **Is** <u>Toon</u> a great artist?

8. (a) <u>We</u> **<u>were</u>** playing soccer yesterday.
    (b) _____

9.   (a)   _____

      (b)   <u>**Are**</u> <u>we</u> allowed to water-ski tomorrow?

10. (a)   <u>People from Chiang Mai</u> <u>**are**</u> great artists.

      (b)   _____

11. (a)   _____

      (b)   <u>**Was**</u> <u>Oi</u> <u>**swimming**</u> yesterday?

12. (a)   <u>Mint</u> <u>**was**</u> sick last week.

      (b)   _____

13. (a)   <u>Bee and Jobim</u> <u>**are**</u> great water-skiers.

      (b)   _____

B—The Verb "Do"

Make sure the tenses and forms of the verbs are correct.

1.   (a)   <u>Peera</u> <u>**likes**</u> to eat pad Thai. (Note how <u>**like**</u> changes form.)

      (b)   <u>**Does**</u> Peera <u>**like**</u> to eat pad Thai?

2.   (a)   <u>Fung</u> <u>**swims**</u> in the ocean every day.

      (b)   _____

3.   (a)   <u>Sun</u> <u>**ate**</u> her vegetables.   (Note how <u>**eat**</u> changes tense.)

      (b)   <u>**Did**</u> Sun <u>**eat**</u> her vegetables?

4.   (a)   <u>**You**</u> <u>**know**</u> Thanadol.

      (b)   _____

5.   (a)   _____

      (b)   <u>**Does**</u> <u>it</u> <u>**rain**</u> in Thailand in the summer?

6.   (a)   <u>Sharks</u> <u>**swim faster**</u> than dolphins.

      (b)   _____

7.   (a)   _____

      (b)   <u>**Does**</u> <u>Tata</u> <u>**like**</u> to water ski?

8. (a) The <u>Dugong</u> **looks like** a manatee.
   (b) _____

9. (a) _____
   (b) **Do** <u>Thai people</u> **like** mangos better than papayas.

10. (a) For some people, the <u>Durian</u> **tastes bitter**.
    (b) _____

11. (a) _____
    (b) **Did** <u>Poon</u> **turn off** the computer last night?

12. (a) <u>Pun</u> **ate** all her dinner last night.
    (b) _____

13. (a) <u>Yes,</u> _____
    <u>No,</u> _____
    (b) **Did** <u>you</u> **eat** all <u>your</u> beans last night, June?

14. (a) The <u>cat</u> **didn't come** home last night.
    (b) _____

B10—Animals

Nouns, Verbs, and Adverbs
Actions and Sounds of Animals

Act out these actions and sounds in class.

Animal	Action Present Tense	Action Past Tense
beaver	gnaw, swim	gnawed, swam
bird	peck, fly	pecked, flew
dog	bark	barked
duck	waddle, quack	waddled, quacked
eagle	dive, fly, hover	dove, flew, hovered
elephant	trumpet, blow water	trumpeted, blew water
frog	croak	croaked
gorilla	thump	thumped
horse	gallop, trot, run, neigh	galloped, trotted, ran, neighed
lion	run, roar, eat, chew	ran, roared, ate, chewed
monkey	climb, swing, chatter	climbed, swung, chattered
owl	hoot	hooted
penguin	strut, waddle	strutted, waddled
pig	wallow, snort	wallowed, snorted
rooster	cackle, crow	cackled, crowed
sheep	bah	bahed
squirrel	chatter, climb, chew	chattered, climbed, chew
wolf	howl	howled
worm	wriggle	wriggled

Definitions - Things That Animals Do

bark	- the short, explosive sound that a dog makes
cackle	- the sound a rooster makes
climb	- to go up or ascend something, like a tree
crow	- the action a rooster does when it says "cock-a-doodle-do"

dive	- to jump or plunge headfirst into the water
fly	- to move through the air like a bird does
howl	- to make a long mournful sound or cry like a wolf or dog does
gallop	- the fast running style of a horse
gnaw	- to bite or chew away at something, little by little
hoot	- the sound made by an owl
hover	- to remain suspended in air above something
neigh	- the noise a horse makes
peck	- to strike or hit something with the beak, like a bird does
quack	- the noise that ducks make
roar	- to make loud noises with the mouth
run	- to move with your feet in a rapid or fast way
snort	- to make short, grunting noises through your nose, like a pig does
swim	- to move through water by moving your arms and/or legs
swing	- to move back and forth
strut	- to walk in a proud way
thump	- to beat or hit your chest rapidly, like a gorilla does
trumpet	- to make a noise like a trumpet, in the same way an elephant does
trot	- the slow running style of a horse
waddle	- to walk with short steps and to move back and forth, like a duck
wallow	- to roll about in the mud, in the same way that a pig does
wriggle	- to squirm on the ground from side to side

In the spaces provided, write down some things that these animals do.

	Animal		Group Name	Action
1.	dolphins	a.	school	dive, _____
2.	lions	b.	pride	_____
3.	squirrels	c.	scurry	_____
4.	birds	d.	flock	_____
5.	elephants	e.	herd	_____
6.	ants	f.	colony	_____

Animal Group Names:

Dolphins swim in **schools**.

The **pride** of lions sat by the river.

A **scurry** of squirrels live in the tree.

Birds fly in **flock**s.

Elephants gather in **herds**.

Ants live in a **colony**.

Practice Exercise 1: Use each verb (once) to complete the sentences.

galloped   **pecked**   **waddled**   **wallowed**   **strutted**

1. The ducks _____ down to the pond.
2. The pigs _____ in the mud.
3. The beautiful peacock proudly _____ about.
4. The horses _____ across the empty field.
5. The chickens _____ at the fresh corn.

barked   **gnawed**   **soared**   **swallowed**   **swung**

6. The eagle <u>soared</u> high into the sky.
7. The hamsters _____ right through the wood.
8. The guard dog _____ loudly.
9. The enormous snake _____ its prey whole.
10. The monkey _____ from tree to tree.

dove   **basked**   **howled**   **hovered**   **swam**

11. The fish _____ in the lake.
12. The hummingbird _____ above the flowers.
13. The wolves _____ throughout the night.
14. The penguins _____ into the icy sea.
15. The crocodile _____ in the midday sun.

climbed   **hooted**   **thumped**   **trumpeted**   **wallowed**

16. The hippopotamus _____ in the muddy water.
17. The squirrel _____ up the tree.
18. The owl _____ in the night.
19. The rabbit _____ the ground with its hind legs.
20. The elephant _____ loudly.

A.   On the Farm with Farm Animals

Place the correct word and the correct tense (present or past) in the spaces.

chirp/chirping	moo/mooing	sing/singing	cackle/cackling

Pigs, cows, horses, chickens, and sheep—these animals all live on a farm. Early in the morning, everyone is awoken by the _____ of the rooster. Then the cows start to _____. After that, all the animals on the farm are heard, so the farm is full of noises. Even the birds, who are not farm animals, begin their _____ and _____.

bah/bahing	cackles/cackling	hoot/hooting	moo/mooing
snort/snorting	wallow/wallowing		

In the barn, the farmer is greeted by the _____ of the cows, the _____ of the sheep, and the _____ of the hens. The pigs are nearby as they _____ in the mud and _____ through their noses. Yes, the farm is a busy place in the morning, as all the animals look forward to being fed—everyone except the owl, who is not _____ but sleeping.

barks/barking	neigh/neighing	gallop/galloping
waddle/waddling	swim/swimming	

Later on in the day, the farm dog shepherds the sheep as he guides the sheep with his _____. The horses _____ around the field as they _____ at each other and jump around. The ducks are _____ in the pond, but then they leave the pond and _____ toward the farmer, who is bringing food for them. Yes, morning is a busy time on the farm as all the animals begin their day.

B. Animals in the Jungle

pride	swing/swinging	trumpet/trumpeting	roar/roaring

Welcome to the jungle. The _____ of an elephant breaks the silence, but there was a reason for the silence: a _____ of lions stands high on the hill, _____ their menacing roar. The monkeys are not afraid, though, because they are high in the trees, _____ on the vines.

dive/dove	wallowing/wallowed	fly/flew	hover/hovering

Other animals also roam the plain, either looking for food or looking for a way to cool down. The hippos are easily spotted as they try to cover themselves with mud by _____ in the muddy lake. The eagles and other birds _____ over the plain as they look for their food for the day. The birds _____ over the dead animals, waiting for their chance to _____ in and get some food for the day.

chatter/chattered climb/climbed sing/sang thump/thumped gallops/galloping

The monkeys _____ when the lions walk by their trees, but lions know they cannot catch a monkey. The parrots are _____ their beautiful songs, but they are safe from the lions as long as they stay in the trees. The lions chase a hyena, but the quick hyena _____ away to safety. It is not a good day for the lions, as they cannot catch any food. The gorillas are standing on another hill, but the lions do not want to challenge a gorilla. The gorillas _____ their chests to show the lions that they are not afraid. If the lions run toward them, the gorillas can _____ the trees, so they will always be safe.

wriggle/wriggled	climbs/climbed	hop/hopped	herd
eat/eaten	trumpet/trumpeting	croak/croaked	

The snakes _____ silently on the ground, trying to find food. A baby monkey falls from his vine, but the mother quickly _____ down the tree and brings the baby back up to safety. A _____ of elephants walks by the trees, but their loud _____ does not frighten the monkeys. All animals in the jungle are hungry, and they are all looking for food, but they also have to be careful, or else they might be _____ by other animals. Meanwhile, the frog swims silently in the water, even though frogs are often known to _____ loudly. Frogs can keep themselves safe, though, because they can quickly _____ away when another animal comes by.

B11—Playing with Elephants

The Verb "To Be"

The verb "to be" is one of the most commonly used verbs in English.

These are the forms of the verb "to be":

Person	Number		Present	Past
first	singular	I	**am**	**was**
second	singular	you	**are**	**were**
third	singular	he / she / it	**is**	**was**
first	plural	we	**are**	**were**
second	plural	you	**are**	**were**
third	plural	they	**are**	**were**

"To be" is a linking verb. It shows the condition of the subject.

Examples:

	<u>Subject</u>	<u>To Be</u>	<u>Object</u> (condition of the subject)
1.	Thanadol	**is**	happy.
2.	Prim	**was**	here earlier.
3.	The girls	**are**	swimming right now.
4.	They	**were**	the winners in the race.
5.	I	**am**	early today.

Practice Exercise: Circle the correct word for each sentence.

1.	Gam	**is / was**	the best student last week.
2.	This test	**was / were**	the easiest test this month.
3.	Earn and Ice	**are / were**	both early this morning.
4.	We	**were / is**	drinking coconut drinks on the beach.
5.	Haddis	**was / are**	drawing a beautiful picture in class.
6.	Pao and Fah	**are / am**	the tallest girls in the school.
7.	Fah	**was / is**	just as tall as Pao.
8.	Keeko	**were / is**	shorter than Pao or Fah
9.	They	**is / were**	practicing for the play all day.

10. Prim   **is / am**   the best swimmer in the school.

The Verb "To Be": Circle the correct form of the verb "to be" in each sentence

1.   Prim   **am / is / are** riding Jumpy.
2.   Jamjalai   **am / is / was** huge.
3.   Jumpy's ears   **were / are / is** big.

 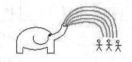

4.   Kulaneet   **am / is / were** feeding Popeye.
5.   Popeye   **is / are / am** spraying us.

6.   The people   **are / is / am** riding the elephants.
7.   There   **was / were / are** five elephants.
8.   The lead elephant **is / were / am** the biggest elephant.

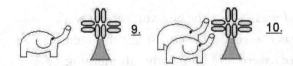

9.   Popeye   **is / am / was** eating bananas.
10. Popeye and Baby   **am / is / are** eating bananas.
11. Popeye and Baby   **am / be / are** side by side.
12. Popeye   **am / be / is** next to Baby.

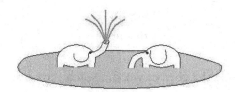

13. Popeye   **is / are / was** spraying water.
14. Baby   **am / is / were** sipping water.
15. Popeye and Baby   **be / are / were** the same size.
16. Popeye and Baby   **be / are / am** face-to-face.
17. Popeye and Baby   **are / is / am** are water lovers.

The Present Tense—Present Continuous

Simple present is used to talk about a current action or something that is done by habit. Present continuous is *only* used to talk about what is *currently happening*.

Example of Present Continuous:

Subject	"To Be" Verb + ing	Object
I	am eat**ing**	dinner.

Present Continuous talks about what is happening at the <u>present time.</u>

Grammar:

Subject	**is** + **Verb** + **ing**	**Object**
Peera	**is** play**ing**	golf now.

Comparisons between the present simple and present continuous:

Present Simple			**Present Continuous**		
I	**play**	golf each week.	I	**am**	**playing** golf now.
Pong	**eats**	pad Thai for lunch.	Pong	**is**	**eating** pad Thai.
Pun	**climbs**	trees every day.	Pun	**is**	**climbing** the tree.
Prim	**loves**	to eat bananas.	Prim	**is**	**eating** a banana.

More examples of **present continuous:**

Subject	Verb "To Be"	Verb + ing	Object
Pun Pun	is	playing	the piano
Kanoon	is	eating	lunch now.
Fah and Tiger	are	playing	basketball.
Pao Pao	is	writing	an essay.

Mek and Pop	are	shopping	at the mall.
Haddis	is	running	up the stairs.

The Present Continuous: Circle the correct word in each sentence.

1. (a) Prim is   **fed / feed / feeding** Popeye.

   (b) Popeye is   **ate / eat / eating** from Prim's hand.

2. (a) Jamjalai is   **raise / raising / raised** his trunk.

   (b) Achita is   **standing / stand / stood** under Jamjali's trunk.

3. Jumpy is   **flap / flapped / flapping** his big ears.

4. (a) Jumpy is   **spray / sprayed / spraying** water on us.

   (b) We are   **stand / standing / stood** under the water.

5. Jobim is   **riding/ ride / rode** behind Peera.

6. The people are   **ride / rode / riding** the elephants.

7. The smaller elephants are   **follow / following / follow** the lead elephant.

8. The big elephant is   **lead / leading / leader** the pack.

9. (a) Popeye is **eat / eats / eating** bananas.
    (b) Popeye is **standing / stands / stood** next to the tree.

10. Popeye and Baby are **eat / eaten / eating** bananas.

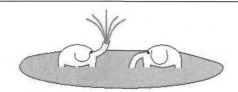

11. Popeye and Baby are   **played / play / playing** in the water.

12. Popeye is   **spray / spraying / sprayed** water.

13. Baby is   **sipping / sip / sipped** water.

14. Popeye and Baby are   **love / loving / love** life.

B12—Thai People and Their Customs

Adverbs of Frequency

Adverbs of frequency express **how often** something happens or is done.

This is a general representation of nine adverbs of frequency:

Always	100 percent (%)
Almost Always	90–95 percent
Usually	
Often	
Sometimes	40–60 percent
Occasionally	
Seldom	
Rarely	5–10 percent
Never	0 percent

Sample sentences using adverbs of frequency:

1.	Americans	**often**	put cream in their coffee.
2.	In China, people	**seldom**	put sugar in their tea.
3.	In England, people	**usually**	have milk with their tea.
4.	In Korea, people	**almost always**	eat kimchi at every meal.
5.	Italian people	**usually**	eat spaghetti.
6.	In Brazil, people	**often**	make drinks with fruit.
7.	Americans	**rarely**	have salad at breakfast.
8.	Canadians	**never**	eat fish for breakfast.
9.	Mexicans	**usually**	eat food like tacos or burritos.
10.	Japanese	**almost always**	eat rice.

Practice Questions

1. What do you   **usually**   eat for **breakfast**?

    I   **usually**   eat _____.

    I   **usually**   eat **cereal**, **milk** and **toast**.

2. What do you   **seldom**   eat for lunch?

    I   **seldom**   eat _____ for lunch.

3. What do you   **always**   eat at **dinner**?

    I   **always**   eat _____.

4. Do you   **ever**   skip **breakfast**?

    No, I   _____   skip **breakfast**.

    Yes, I   _____   skip **breakfast**.

5. Do you   **often**   eat **lunch** at a **restaurant**?

    No, I   _____   eat **lunch** at a **restaurant**.

    Yes, I   _____   eat **lunch** at a **restaurant**.

    Well, I   _____   eat **lunch** at a **restaurant**.

6. Do you   **usually**   have **coffee** for **breakfast**?

    No, I   _____   drink **coffee** for **breakfast**.

    Yes, I   _____   drink **coffee** for **breakfast**.

    Well, I   _____   drink **coffee** for **breakfast**.

7. Do you   **ever**   eat **yogurt**?

    I   _____   eat **yogurt**.

8. Do you   **ever**   eat ice cream for dessert?

    I   _____   eat ice cream for dessert?

Thai People and Adverbs of Frequency

Place a suitable adverb of frequency in the blanks below.

1. Thai people _____**rarely**_____ ride their elephant to work.
2. Thai food is _____**usually**_____ spicy.
3. Monks _____ wear shoes.
4. Thai people _____ ride their bikes to work.
5. Thai people _____ eat at sidewalk food stalls.
6. People in Bangkok _____ take a river taxi or riverboat ride to cross a river.
7. Elephants _____ flap their ears to cool themselves down.
8. A baby elephant is _____ very cute and loveable.
9. Thai people _____ eat pad Thai every day.
10. Thai beaches are _____ very crowded, because they are very beautiful, and they have fine white sand on them.
11. Thai people _____ take rides in tuk-tuks.
12. Northern hill tribes _____ live in jungles.
13. Thai people _____ like to eat American-style fast foods.
14. Monkeys are _____ respected in Thailand because of the popularity of Hanuman, the Monkey Warrior.
15. Foreigners _____ like to go on elephant safaris when they visit Thailand.
16. Thais _____ celebrate the annual Son Klang Festival in Thailand.
17. Thai people _____ respect their king and queen.
18. The rice festival is _____ held in Bangkok's Sanum Luang Grounds, every May.
19. The Phallic is an ornament with a figure of a monkey, lizard, or woman emblazoned on it. It is _____ waved at men, by women, during Isan rain-making rites.
20. Most Thai women _____ watch Thai kickboxing.
21. Thai people _____ drive on the left side of the road.
22. Many women _____ like shopping at MBK (Mah Boon Krong) in Bangkok.
23. Hunters on the Mekong _____ used to paint figures of animals on the cliffs because they believed this would bring good luck.
24. The hunters _____ mixed tree gum with red soil and animal fat to make the paint.

25. Thai children _____ drink alcohol.
26. The best art was _____ painted inside the palaces of the kings and queens in ancient Thailand.
27. The sleeping Buddha is _____ lying down..
28. The sleeping Buddha _____ stands up.
29. Thai wats _____ have a round roof.
30. The Floating Market is _____ crowded with shoppers.
31. Thai children _____ wear uniforms to school.
32. Thai people _____ like to give offerings to monks.
33. Thai kids _____ love coconut drinks.

B13—Questions about Thailand

"Wh" Questions

Wh Questions—Who, Whose, Which, Where, When, What, Why, How

Wh questions are among the most common types of questions asked.

(Please refer to **Appendix E**, Page 225 - 226, for an explantion on **Wh** Questions, and an explanation on the reason that **HOW** is included as a **Wh** Question)

Use	To Ask About	Sentences
who	people other identifying information	Who is she? Who does this car belong to?
whose	ownership possession	Whose book is this?
which	preference	Which teacher is your favorite?
where	location places	Where is Bangkok? Where is your school?
when	time (in general)	When is the party?
what time	time (specific)	What time does the game start?
why	reasons	Why are you studying ESL?
what ... for	reasons	What did you study ESL for?
how	reasons	How do you operate this smartphone?
how much how many	quantity	How much sugar do you use? How many cups do you have?
how long	duration; time length	How long does the test last? How long is her dress?

Sample Sentences:

		Question	**Answer**
1.	**Who**	<u>Who</u> are you? <u>Who</u> does this book belong to?	I am the new student. That book is mine.
2.	**Whose**	<u>Whose</u> book is this?	That book is mine.

3.	**Which**	<u>Which</u> color do you like?	I like red.

4.	**Where**	<u>Where</u> is my book?	Prim borrowed it.
		<u>Where</u> is Bangkok?	Bangkok is in Thailand.
		<u>Where</u> will we eat lunch?	At my house.

5.	**When**	<u>When</u> will you go to Phuket?	Next week.
		<u>When</u> will school finish?	At noon.

6.	**What time**	<u>What time</u> will school finish?	At noon.
		<u>What time</u> is it?	It is three o'clock.

7.	**Why**	<u>Why</u> are you going home now?	I feel sick.
		You dropped the flower vase.	
		<u>Why</u> did you do that?	It was an accident.

8.	**What … for**	You dropped the flower vase.	
		<u>What</u> did you do that <u>for</u>?	It was an accident.
		<u>What</u> did you go to Thailand <u>for</u>?	To teach English.

9.	**How**	<u>How</u> did you get an A?	I studied very hard.
		<u>How</u> do you turn on the light?	Turn the switch on.

10. (a) **How much**

		<u>How much</u> money do you have?	I have five hundred baht.
		<u>How much</u> longer must we wait?	About thirty minutes.
		<u>How much</u> pad Thai did you eat?	I ate one bowl of pad Thai.

Much is used for <u>noncount nouns</u>, such as **money, air,** and **blood.**

(b) **How many**

		<u>How many</u> coconuts do you have?	I have five coconuts.
		<u>How many</u> birds do you see?	I see ten birds.

Many is used for <u>count nouns</u> like **apples, trees,** and **bicycles.**

11.	**How long**	<u>How long</u> have you lived in Trat?	For five years.
		<u>How long</u> is your foot?	Fifteen centimeters long.

Practice Exercises

Choose the correct "wh" question from the parentheses and write it in the blank.

1. (**How / How long**) _____ have you lived in Chang Mai?

2. (**Where / How**) _____ is Phet Kasem Road?

3. **(Who / Whose)** _____ tuk-tuk is that?

4. **(How / How long)** _____ is Suchera's hair?

5. **(When time / What time)** _____ is lunch today?

6. **(When / What)** _____ will we go swimming today?

7. **(Where / How)** _____ far is Ko Chang from Bangkok?

8. **(How long / How)** _____ is the football field?

9. **(How much / How many)** _____ pad Thai do you want?

10. **(Why / How long)** _____ is the elephant's trunk?

11. **(Which / Why)** _____ student did the best in the test?

Main Exercise: Make questions from the sentences below.

1. **Sentence**

   Elephants love to eat sugarcane.

   Questions
   Which animal loves to eat sugarcane?
   What animal loves to eat sugarcane?
   What do elephants love to eat?

2. Phuket is in the southern part of Thailand.

   _____

   _____

3. Elephants flap their ears to cool themselves down.

   _____

   _____

4. A tsunami is a big wave in the ocean.

   _____

   _____

5. Thailand is in Southeast Asia.

_____

_____

6. A wat is a Buddhist Thai temple.

_____

_____

7. The sun sets at seven o'clock in Thailand, every day of the year.

_____

_____

8. King Rama IX (or Blumibol) is the present king of Thailand.

_____

_____

9. Sixty-six million people live in Thailand.

_____

_____

10. The Thai king, Rama IX, celebrated his eightieth birthday in

_____

_____

11. In 2006, King Rama IX celebrated his fiftieth anniversary on the throne.

_____

_____

12. A person in Thailand can go to jail for seven years for criticizing the king.

_____

_____

13. Most Thais practice the Theravada Buddhist type of religion.

_____

_____

14. Ayuttyaha was the capital of Thailand before

_____

_____

15. The Hi-So is made up of the Thai nobility and wealthy Sino-Thai families.

_____

_____

16. Thais greet each other by bowing and then by executing a *wai*.

_____

_____

17. A person executes a wai by clasping their hands together in front of them.

_____

_____

18. Buddha is the symbol of Thai Buddhism.

_____

_____

19. Most of Thailand's monks live in wats.

_____

_____

20. There are about 300,000 monks in Thailand.

_____

_____

B14—Thai Kids at the Beach

Simple Present and Present Continuous

We will look at two **present** verb tenses:

    (1)   Simple present

    (2)   Present continuous

(1) Simple Present   Used to talk about things people do each day or things people do by habit

Grammar:	**Subject**	**Verb**	**Object**	
	Prim	plays	golf	every day.

(2) Present Continuous   Used to talk about things people are doing at the present time

Grammar:	**Subject**	**is** + **Verb** + **ing**	**Object**
	Peera	**is** play**ing**	golf now.

Subject / Verb Agreement

Using the correct form of the verb is important in the present tense.

Examples—Simple Present—Subject/Verb Agreement

The elephant **likes** bananas   The elephant**s** **like** bananas.
I **like** to climb trees.   We **like** to climb trees.
Peera **plays** golf every day.   Peera and Job **play** golf every day.
The boy **swims** every day.   The boys **swim** every day.

Grammar for Simple Present

	Subject	Verb		Form of Verb
(A)	I, You, They, We	**eat**	pad Thai.	verb is **singular**
(B)	She, He, Prim	**eats**	pad Thai.	verb is **plural**

Examples—Present Continuous—Subject/Verb Agreement

The <u>girl</u> **is** swimm**ing**.   The girl**s** **are** swimm**ing**.
The <u>monkey</u> **is** climb**ing** the tree.   The monkey**s** **are** climb**ing** the trees.
The <u>boy</u> **is** play**ing** golf now.   The boy**s** **are** play**ing** golf now.

Grammar for Present Continuous

	Subject	Verb To Be		Form of Verb To Be
(C)	I	am	eating pad Thai.	am
(D)	She, He, Prim	is	eating pad Thai.	is
(E)	They, We, You	are	eating pad Thai.	are

Practice Exercise 1: Choose the correct verb tense.

1. The teacher (**mark / marks**) <u>marks </u>our tests very hard.

2. The students (**is / are**) _____ **napping** now.

3. Atte (**nap / naps**) _____ every day in school.

4. The rabbits (**is / are**) _____ **eating** carrots.

5. He (**want / wants**) _____ to go home.

6. They (**want / wants**) _____ to go to school.

7. The cat often (**jump / jumps**) _____ all over the place.

8. The students (**is / are**) _____ wearing their scout uniforms to school today.

9. Pao (**is / are**) _____ **wearing** her uniform at home.

10. Kanoon (**run / runs**) _____ home every day.

11. The teacher is (**give / giving**) _____ the students a test.

12. Cartoon (**is / are**) _____ **wearing** her scout hat.

Practice Exercise 2: Subject/Verb Agreement
Choose the correct verb in the sentences

1. My friends (**is / are**) _____ coming to my house today.

2. I (**go/went**) _____ to the beach yesterday.

3. I will (**go/went**) _____ to the beach tomorrow.

4. Prim (**am / is**) _____ a girl.

5. I (**am/ are**) _____ fourteen years old

6. Thanodol (**was / is**) _____ late today.

7. Thabodol (**was / is**) _____ late yesterday.

8. The picture near the stairs (**is / are**) _____ beautiful.

Thai Kids at the Beach

Main Exercise: Choose the correct word from the parentheses.

1. Sanitol (**is / are**) _____ **munching** on a pineapple.

2. Prim (**is / are**) _____ **flying** a kite.

3. Fah and Jane (**played / plays**) _____ computer

4. games in their hotel in the evening.

5. Taj (**is / are**) _____ **drinking** a coconut drink.

6. Tata (**is / are**) _____ **singing** a song, and Minh (**is / are**) _____ **playing** her guitar under the palm tree.

7. Tata (**sing / sings**) _____ very well.

8. Toon and Fah (**are / is**) also _____ **singing** along.

9. Fah (**is / are**) _____ **singing** the loudest.

10. Fah (**sing / sings**) _____ very well.

11. Fah's name (**is / are**) _____ **appearing** in many sentences.

12. Mee likes to (**eat / eats**) _____ papayas at the beach.

13. Tul (**is / are**) _____ **learning** how to ride a Jet Ski.

14. Poom (**is / are**) _____ **dreaming** about her last vacation.

15. Khae is (**shop / shopping**) _____ at the market on the beach.

16. The jungle boy (**is / are**) _____ **riding** an elephant.

17. Pung Pung (**was / were**) _____ **sliding down** the waterslide.

18. Keeko (**love / loves**) _____ octopus on a stick.

19. Dream (**want / wants**) _____ pepperoni pizza instead of octopus on a stick.

20. Prim is (**takes / taking**) _____ pictures of the dolphins.

21. Prang doesn't (**want / wants**) _____ to go home.

22. Bamh (**is / are**) _____ **surfing**.

23. Mook (**is / are**) _____ **paragliding**.

11—My Holiday in Phuket

Expressions of Time and Verb Tenses

Expressions of time and verb tenses are studied in this lesson.

You are in Phuket from Monday to Friday. Below are your planned activities. The verbs are in the **present tense**. Review the verbs.

Monday

10:00 a.m.	**Ride** an elephant.
Noon	**Feed** elephants sugarcane and bananas and then **pet** them.
1:00 p.m.	**Take** a bus to Kata Beach.
2:00 p.m.	**Relax** on Kata Beach for a few hours.
4:00 p.m.	**Windsurf** for two hours.
6:00 p.m.	**Take** a bus back to Patong Beach.
7:00 p.m.	**Eat** octopus on a stick.
8:00 p.m.	**Drink** a big coconut drink out of a coconut shell.

Tuesday

11:00 a.m.	**Rent** scuba gear.
Noon	**Go** scuba diving. **See** many beautiful fish, flora, and fauna on the reef. **Take** pictures with a waterproof camera.
4:00 p.m.	**Watch** the dolphins **jump** in and out of the water.
6:00 p.m.	**Eat** a spicy Thai dish of Tom Yam.
7:00 p.m.	**Wade** in the cool water.
8:00 p.m.	**Drink** cold drinks on the beachfront.
9:00 p.m.	**Walk** on the beach.
10:00 p.m.	**Listen** to music that is being **played** by street entertainers.

Wednesday

9:00 a.m.	**Go** on a tour of Krabi.
	See many beautiful mountains on the bus ride to Krabi.
11:00 a.m.	**Visit** the Hot Springs Waterfall before reaching Krabi.
1:00 p.m.	**Go** rock climbing at Railay Bay.
3:00 p.m.	**Visit** Wat Tham Sena.

5:00 p.m.	**Ride** in a glass-bottom boat on Maya Bay. **Drink** coconut juice out of a coconut shell. **See** beautiful fish swim under the boat.
	Jump into the water from the boat and **swim** for a while.
7:00 p.m.	**Arrive** back on shore. **Wade** around in the water.
8:00 p.m.	**Take** the bus back to Phuket.
9:00 p.m.	**Eat** a spicy Thai meal.

Thursday

10:00 a.m.	**Shop** at a shopping mall. **Have** a pineapple drink out of the shell. **Buy** souvenirs.
Noon	**Eat** lunch on the beach.
2:00 p.m.	**Rent** a surfboard. **Surf** for a few hours.
4:00 p.m.	**Relax** on the beach. **Watch** dolphins **play** in the water.
6:00 p.m.	**Eat** pizza at a pizza restaurant.
7:00 p.m.	**Go** to Phuket Fantasea, Phuket's theme park.
	Watch acrobats, traditional Thai dancers, and fireworks.

Friday

Noon	**Sleep** in until noon. **Eat** spicy Thai food for lunch.
1:00 p.m.	**Rent** a motorcycle.
	Ride around the island of Phuket.
2:00 p.m.	**Arrive** at the east side of Phuket island. **Tour** the small towns.
3:00 p.m.	**Rent** a mask and **snorkel** in the waters of Ko Racha.
6:00 p.m.	**Eat** octopus on a stick. **Drink** pineapple juice out of a pineapple.
7:00 p.m.	**Drive** back to Patong.
8:00 p.m.	**Arrive** in Patong. **Eat** burgers and fries.
9:00 p.m.	**Walk** on the beach, then **sit** down for a few hours to **take in** the cool breezes from the ocean.

Time Expressions

In this lesson, you will talk about what you did on certain days. You will talk about these things in the **past, present, or future**. These <u>expressions of time</u> will be used to do this:

When talking about the **previous day**, use the following expressions:

| yesterday | yesterday morning | yesterday afternoon | last night |

When talking about the **present day**, use the following expressions:

a few minutes ago	**a few hours ago**	**in a few hours**	**in an hour**
in a few minutes	**this morning / afternoon / evening**		**tonight**

When talking about the **next day**, use the following expressions:

tomorrow morning	**tomorrow afternoon**	**tomorrow night**
in a few days	**on the next day**	

Students will be asked to talk about the <u>itinerary</u> of a **specific day**, from the <u>perspective</u> of a **different day**.

Example: It is **Wednesday**. Talk about what you **did** on **Tuesday**.

Tuesday—Original Description—Present Tense

11:00 a.m.	**Rent** scuba gear.
Noon	**Go** scuba diving. **See** many beautiful fish, flora, and fauna on the reef. **Take** pictures with a waterproof camera.
4:00 p.m.	**Watch** the dolphins **jump** in and out of the water.
6:00 p.m.	**Eat** a spicy Thai dish of Tom Yam.
7:00 p.m.	**Wade** in the cool water.
8:00 p.m.	**Drink** cold drinks on the beachfront.
9:00 p.m.	**Walk** on the beach.
10:00 p.m.	**Listen** to music that **is** being **played** by street entertainers.

It is now **Wednesday**. Talk about what you **did** on **Tuesday**.

11:00 a.m.	I **rented** scuba gear **yesterday morning**.
Noon	Then I **went** scuba diving **yesterday** at noon. I **saw** many beautiful fish, and many flora and fauna on the reef. I **took** many pictures of the fish with my waterproof camera.
4:00 p.m.	I **watched** dolphins jump in and out of the water **yesterday afternoon**.
6:00 p.m.	I **ate** a spicy Thai dish of Tom Yam **last night**.
7:00 p.m.	I **waded** in the cool beach water **after that**.
8:00 p.m.	I **drank** cold drinks on the beachfront **at 8:00 p.m. last night**.
9:00 p.m.	I **walked** on the beach.
10:00 p.m.	I **listened** to music that **was** being **played** by street entertainers.

The following past-tense verbs were used in this sample exercise:

Verb Type	Past Tense	Present Tense
Regular	rented	rent
R	waded	wade
R	watched	watch
R	listened	listen
R	played	play
Irregular	went	go
I	saw	see
I	took	take
I	ate	eat
I	drank	drink

Regular Verbs

When forming the past tense of a regular verb, **add** "ed" to the end.

Irregular Verbs

There are no set rules for forming the past tense for irregular verbs. To form the past tense of irregular verbs, look up the verb in verb tables.

Future: Use the words **will** or **be going to** to talk about the future.

In question 4, for example, you must use **verbs** in the future tense.

Example:

4.   I **will** **go shopping** tomorrow morning. Then I'm **going to have** a coconut drink from the coconut. After that, I **will** buy souvenirs.

Note: Use words like then and after that to make sentences flow naturally.

List of Regular Verbs		
Past Tense	**Present Tense**	**Future Tense**
arrived	arrive	arrive
jumped	jump	jump
listened	listen	listen
petted	pet	pet

played	play	play
relaxed	relax	relax
rented	rent	rent
shopped	shop	shop
snorkeled	snorkel	snorkel
toured	tour	tour
visited	visit	visit
waded	wade	wade
watched	watch	watch
walked	walk	walk
windsurfed	windsurf	windsurf

Present Tense

I **play** volleyball every day.

I like to **windsurf**.

Past Tense

I **played** volleyball last night.

I **windsurfed** a lot last week.

Add "**ed**" to the end of the verb to change the tense to past tense.

List of Irregular Verbs		
Past Tense	**Present Tense**	**Future Tense**
bought	buy	buy
drank	drink	drink
drove	drive	drive
ate	eat	eat
fed	feed	feed
went	go	go
had	have	have
rode	ride	ride
saw	see	see
sat	sit	sit
slept	sleep	sleep
swam	swim	swim
took	take	take

<u>Present Tense</u>
I usually **sleep** eight hours each day.
I **drink** coconut drinks at lunch.

<u>Past Tense</u>
I only **slept** six hours last night.
I **drank** two coconut drinks yesterday.

There are **no** set rules when forming the <u>past tense</u> of irregular verbs.

Do these exercises based on the way the sample lesson was done.

1. It is now **Monday, 6:00 p.m.** Talk about <u>what you did</u>, <u>what you are doing</u>, or <u>what you will do</u> on **Monday**, using the appropriate expressions of time.

2. It is now **Wednesday**. Talk about what you did on **Tuesday**.

3. It is now **Monday**. Talk about what you will do **Friday**.

4. It is now **Wednesday**. Talk about what you will do on **Thursday**.

5. It is now **Friday**. Talk about what you did on **Wednesday**.

6. Make up some of your own scenarios, based on the itineraries above.

7. Make up some of your own scenarios, based on things you do every day in your life.

12—A Day at the Beach

Present Tense

There are four **present verb tenses** in the English language:

Present Simple
Present Continuous
Present Perfect
Present Perfect Continuous

1. **Present Simple (PS)**

   Describes present activities or talks about routines or habits.

   Grammar: subject + **verb** + object

   Examples: I   **live** in Ayuttyaha.
                Toon   **brushes** her teeth every morning.

2. **Present Continuous (PC)**

   Expresses the idea that something is happening at the moment.

   Grammar: subject +   **is/are/am** + **verb** (continuous form)

   Examples: Bam   **is**   **sleeping**.
                I   **am**   **going** to class now.

3. **Present Perfect (PP)**

   Used to talk about actions that happened at an **indefinite time** in the past and that continue on into the present.

   Grammar: subject + **has/have** + **verb**

   Examples: I   **have**   **lived** in Trat for a long time.

4. **Present Perfect Continuous (PPC)**

   Used to talk about actions that happened at a **definite time** in the past and that continue on into the present.

Grammar: subject + **has/have** + **been** + **verb**

Examples: Krit   **has**   **been living** at home for twenty-five years.
              I   **have**   **been studying** for ten hours.

Practice Exercise

Choose the correct tense for the sentences. Refer to the diagram for help.

PS   –   Present Simple
PC   –   Present Continuous
PP   –   Present Perfect
PPC   –   Present Perfect Continuous

1. The jungle boy **has been riding** elephants since he was young. **PP**

2. The jungle boy **has been riding** elephants for five years. _____

3. Pam **is snorkeling** in the cool water. _____

4. The sun **is shining** brightly. _____

5. Coconuts **are** delicious. _____

6. Sue **drinks** a lot of coconut juice. _____

7. Sue **has been drinking** coconut juice since she was a baby. _____

8. Sue **has been drinking** coconut juice for seven years. _____

9. Jim **has been tanning** on this beach for a long time. _____

10. The bird did not **drop** the rock on the hill. _____

11. The bird **is soaring** through the sky. _____

12. The jungle boy **cools off** whenever his elephant sprays water on him. _____

13. People **have been fascinated** by Thailand's dolphins for many, many years. _____

14. The baby elephant **has been going** to the beach for two years. _____

15. Monkeys like to **climb** trees. _____

Present Simple: This exercise uses the **present simple** tense. Place the **verbs** in the correct blanks. Refer to the picture.

climb	**drink**	**drink**	**fall**	**glide**	**lies**
loves	**paraglides**	**ride**	**ride**	**roll**	**snorkels**
spray	**swim**				

1. Pam **snorkels**_____ every day.

2. The jungle boy likes to _____ the elephant.

3. Coconuts often _____ off trees.

4. It is dangerous to stand at the bottom of the hill when rocks _____ down the hill.

5. Birds like to _____ in the air.

6. Monkeys often _____ trees to get the coconuts.

7. Sue likes to _____ coconut juice on a hot day.

8. The mother elephant doesn't need to help the baby elephant when it wants to _____ some water.

9. The brave man is not afraid to _____ a dolphin.

10. John _____ on windy days.

11. A lot of fish _____ near the surface in Thailand.

12. Jim _____ on the beach each to get a good tan.

13. The sun _____ when there are no clouds.

14. The big elephant loves to _____ others with water.

Present Continuous: This exercise uses the **present continuous** tense. Place the **verbs** in the correct blanks. Refer to the picture.

climbing	**drinking**	**falling**	**floating**	**flying**
jumping	**lying**	**paragliding**	**riding**	**riding**
rolling	**sipping**	**snorkeling**	**spraying**	**swimming**

1. The coconut is **falling** off the tree.

2. The jungle boy is _____ the elephant.

3. The bird is _____ over the tree.

4. The elephant is _____ water on the dolphin.

5. The monkey is _____ the tree.

6. The rock is _____ down the hill.

7. The girl in the water is _____.

8. The boy is _____ on the beach.

9. The baby elephant is _____ water.

10. The dolphin is _____ out of the water.

11. The girl is _____ coconut milk.

12. The man is _____ the dolphin.

13. The man in the air is _____.

14. The sun is _____ over the jungle boy.

15. The fish is _____ in the water.

13—Geographical Use of the Word "the" and Other Uses of "The"

You will learn the correct way to use the word **the**.

1. **Don't** use the word **the** with geographical nouns.

- **most countries** Italy, Thailand, Mexico
  exceptions: the United States, the Philippines, the Dominican Republic

  Don't say, "the Italy" or "the Mexico."
  Do say, "the United States" or "the Philippines."

- **cities** Bangkok, Vancouver, Paris
  Don't say, "the Bangkok."

- **lakes** Lake Erie, Lake Louise
  exception: the Great Lakes

- **continents** North America
- **islands** Easter Island, Key West
  exceptions: island chains the Aleutian Islands

- **mountains** Mount Everest, Grouse Mountain
  exceptions: mountain ranges the Rockies

Don't say, the Thailand, the Malaysia, the Canada, the Bangkok, the Asia, the Mount Everest, the North America.

2. **Do** use the word **the** with:

- oceans, rivers, seas the Pacific Ocean, the Andaman Sea
- points on the globe the North Pole, the equator
- geographical areas the Middle East
- gulfs, deserts, forests the Persian Gulf, the Gobi Desert

3. **Don't** use the word **the** with:

- languages Thai, English, Spanish
- sports names basketball, football
- academic subjects math, biology, English

Incorrect—Don't Say:	Correct—Do Say:
I speak the English.	I speak English.
I am playing the basketball.	I am playing basketball.
I study the math.	I study Math.

Examples

1. Don't use the word **the** with geographical nouns.
(a) I visited Phuket on my trip to Thailand.   **correct**
    I visited **the** Phuket on my trip to Thailand.   **Incorrect   xxx**
(b) Thailand is in Southeast Asia.   **correct**
    Thailand is in **the** Southeast Asia.   **Incorrect   xxx**
2. Do use the word **the** with seas.
    Thailand lies close to **the** China Sea.   **correct**
    Thailand lies close to China Sea.   **Incorrect   xxx**
3. Don't use the word **the** with languages.
    Jenny speaks Italian.   **correct**
    Jenny speaks **the** Italian.   **Incorrect   xxx**

Practice Exercise: Place the word **the** in the blank space if needed. If **the** is not needed, leave the space blank.

1. Connor went swimming in _____ Phuket last week.

2. The island of _____ Ko Samui is very beautiful.

3. _____ Ayuttyaha has many ancient temples.

4. Cambodia lies on _____ Thailand's eastern border.

5. Thailand's southern body of water is _____ Gulf of Thailand.

6. Hat Yai is in _____ south of Thailand.

7. My flight was from _____ Vancouver to _____ Bangkok.

8. We went on a glass-bottom boat at _____ Krabi.

9. Thailand's hill tribes live in _____ northern part of Thailand.

10. Myanmar lies on _____ southern border with Thailand.

11. The fishing is great on _____ Andaman Sea.

12. _____ Than Mayon waterfall is on Ko Chang.

13. I believe _____ Ko Chang has the best beach in the world.

14. _____ Ko Chang archipelago includes the tiny island of _____ Ko Wai.

15. _____ Chang Mai is a city known for its arts and crafts.

16. The southernmost island in _____ Ko Chang archipelago is _____ Ko Kut.

17. _____ Sukhothai is an ancient city that is very well known for its ancient city walls.

18. _____ Mae Hong Son province is well known for the Padaung, whose women wear brass neck rings.

19. _____ Nong Han district in eastern _____ Udon Thani province has the most famous archeological site in _____ Thailand.

20. _____ Phuket has many resort hotels.

21. _____ James Bond Island, close to _____ Krabi, is a favorite place for tourists to visit.

22. _____ Ko Ping Kan is better known as _____ James Bond Island.

23. _____ Mekong River straddles Thailand's northern border.

24. _____ Thailand is a fifteen-hour flight from _____ U.S.

25. Most people in Thailand speak _____ Thai language.

26. _____ Chatuchak Weekend Market is a favorite place for _____ Thais to shop.

27. The Kirimaya luxury boutique resort is close to _____ Haew Narok Waterfalls in _____ Hao Yai National Park.

28. _____ Roi Et, a farming village, is centered on _____ Lake Beung Phlan Chai.

29. The twin bays of _____Ao Thong Nai Pan Noi and _____ Ao Thong Nai Pan Yai lie on the east coast of Thailand.

Main Exercise: Choose at least ten geographical terms. Make sentences with these terms. Put **the** before the word if needed; do not put **the** if not needed.

<u>Example</u>: I lived in Bangkok, but then I moved to _____ Hua Hin because I wanted to live on **the** Gulf of Thailand.

the → **not needed** for Bangkok and Hua Hin
  → **needed** for Gulf of Thailand

14—Eating Thai Food

Past tense of Regular and Irregular Verbs

Regular Verbs: Some examples are **cook, spray,** and **want.**
When forming the past tense of a **regular** verb, just add **ed** to the end of the word.

Present Tense	**cook**	**spray**	**want**
Past Tense	**cooked**	**sprayed**	**wanted**

Present Tense: I **work** eight hours a day.
  I like to **play** basketball.

Past Tense: I **worked** eight hours yesterday.
  I **played** basketball every day last week.

Irregular Verbs: Some examples are **eat, go,** and **swim.**

When forming the past tense of an **irregular** verb, **ed** <u>is not</u> added to the end of the word. Instead, the ending of an **irregular** verb follows no set rule or pattern.

Present Tense	**eat**	**go**	**swim**
Past Tense	**ate**	**went**	**swam**

Present Tense: I **eat** lunch at noon.
  I **swim** each day.

Past Tense: I **ate** lunch at 1:00 p.m. yesterday.
  I only **swam** three times last week.

For some words that end in **y**, change the **y** to **i** and then add **ed** to the end of the word.

	Present Tense	Past Tense
Examples:	hurry	hurried
	study	studied

For a few other words that end in **y**, <u>do not</u> change the **y** to **i**.

	Present Tense	Past Tense
Examples:	stay	stayed
	play	played

Practice—Irregular Verbs: Change the verb from the present to the past tense:

1. Stumpy the whale **(swim)** _____ in the ocean.

2. Miga **(sit)** _____ down on the chair.

3. The birds **(fly)** _____ south to the warmer weather.

4. Amy **(leave)** _____ class early the other day.

5. Lisa **(come)** _____ from Canada a few years ago.

Practice Exercises—Regular Verbs—Past Tense

1. Bosley the elephant **(spray)** _____ water on the people.

2. The panda **(want)** _____ to eat bamboo, but there was none left.

3. Vincent **(study)** _____ hard for the exam.

4. The dugong **(play)** _____ in the water with the small fish.

5. The monkey **(climb)** _____ the tree to get the coconut.

Main Exercise: Change the present tense verb in the parentheses to the past tense.
Note that 1, 4, 7, 11, 12, 13, 14, 15, 16, 17, 18, 19, 20, 21, and 22 use irregular verbs.

1. Mook **(eat)** _____ five cookies yesterday.

2. Kanoon **(taste)** _____ Tom Yan for the first time yesterday.

3. Prang **(nap)** _____ after she ate a big lunch.

4. Prim **(have)** _____ dinner late last night.

5. Krit **(munch)** _____ on pineapple on a stick.

6. The candies **(taste)** _____ very good.

7. Suchera **(guzzle)** _____ down the cool coconut drink, because she **(have)** _____ been playing in the hot sun.

8. The elephant **(sip)** _____ water from the cool lake.

9. Pam **(sip)** _____ her cool pineapple juice while she **(wade)** _____ around in the hotel pool.

10. The jungle boy (**stop**) _____ riding his elephant so he could get a cool drink.

11. My mother (**make**) _____ me a delicious bowl of pad Thai.

12. I (**wake**) _____ up early this morning so that I could have a delicious breakfast with fresh eggs that the chicken (**lay**)_____.

13. After the classes (**finish**) _____ for the day, we (**go**) _____ to get some delicious ice cream.

14. My mother (**make**) _____ a delicious pie, but when she put it outside to cool down, a monkey (**eat**) _____ it all.

15. I (**eat**) _____ a lot of food at the party, but I didn't eat much chicken because it (**be**) _____ too spicy for me.

16. Yesterday at the beach, a lot of people (**be**) _____ eating octopus on a stick.

17. My mother (**go**) _____ to Damnoen Saduak Floating Market yesterday, where she (**buy**) _____ a lot of delicious fruits.

18. Halo halo is my favorite drink. It is (**make**) _____ out of red beans, jackfruit, coconut jellies, ice cream, ice, and cream.

19. Monks must eat their food before noon, so the monk (**get**) _____ his offerings early this morning.

20. The monk in the small village (**paddle**) _____ his canoe down the river and (**get**) _____ his offerings from the people on the riverbank. Then he (**eat**) _____ his meal before noon.

21. The store owner (**offer**) _____ food to the monk.

22. The Mlarbi women (**wake**) _____ up early today and then (**go**) _____ to the jungle where they (**gather**)_____ many edible roots and fruits.

15—At Safari World

Conjunctions—Connecting Words

Conjunctions are words that connect or join two ideas together.

Examples:

(1) I like pizza **and** cola.   **And** is a conjunction.
(2) I don't like cold weather, **but** I do like to ski.   **But** is a conjunction.

Conjunctions can be grouped in the following ways:

To add an idea	**and, also, moreover, in addition, in addition to, besides** I want pad Thai <u>and</u> a coconut drink. <u>In addition to</u> having a lot of shopping malls, Bangkok also has many markets.
To show contrast	**but, however, on the other hand, in contrast** I love living in Bangkok, <u>but</u> sometimes it's too hot for me.
To show similarity	**similar, similarly, likewise** The beach at Kata is <u>similar</u> to the beach at Ko Samet.
To present a choice	**or, but** Do you want Tom Yang <u>or</u> pad Thai for dinner?
To indicate result	**so, therefore, as a result, thus, consequently** I didn't call my mother last week, <u>so</u> she called me.
To indicate unexpected results	**however, still, nevertheless** Even though it rained, we <u>still</u> played soccer.
To indicate reason	**for, because** I live in Krabi <u>because</u> I love its beaches.

Practice Exercises

Choose the correct **conjunction** for each sentence.

1. I didn't study much; (**therefore / because**) _____ I failed the test.

2. Would you like to eat lunch now (**so / or**) _____ later?

3. (**In addition to / Likewise**) _____ baseball, I also like basketball.

88

4. I wanted to go to Phuket with my family this week, **(in contrast / but)** _____ I had to attend an important conference instead.

5. I don't eat fast food anymore, **(because / since)** _____ I must lose weight.

6. I didn't study for my math, **(so / and)** _____ I failed. **(Therefore / Besides)** _____ I am taking math in summer school.

7. Do you prefer a soft drink **(or / also)** _____ a glass of water?

8. Dolphins are very intelligent. **(In contrast / Moreover)**, _____ they will not harm humans.

9. I don't have enough money to go to the concert. **(Likewise / Besides)**, _____ I don't like the type of music that band plays.

10. I drank too much coconut juice today, **(so / because)** _____ my tummy is sore.

11. I really liked riding Popeye the elephant when I went to Ayuttyaha. **(On the other hand / Also)**, _____ I didn't have enough time to see all the magnificent wats in that city.

12. Popeye is my favorite elephant, **(similar / but)** _____ all the other elephant friends of Popeye were fun to play with too.

13. The hotel we stayed in at Kata was comfortable, **(and / similarly)** _____ it also had a pool.

14. I didn't put suntan lotion on today. **(As a result / Because)** _____, I've got a sunburn.

15. My mother works hard **(for / still)** _____ me **(because / thus)** _____ she wants me to go to university.

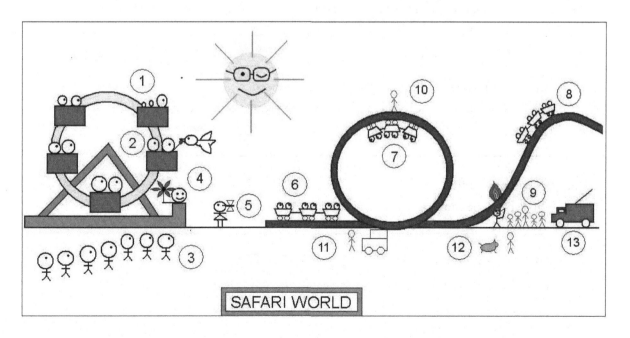

Refer to the drawing to complete the exercises below.

Main Exercise: Join the separate sentences together with a conjunction. By doing this, you will make one sentence.

Example: (a) I'm a girl.
                (b) I like to play soccer.

                I'm a girl, **and** I like to play soccer.

1. (a)   Three of the carriages on the Ferris wheel have two people in them.
    (b)   One carriage on the Ferris wheel has three people in it.

          <u>Three of the carriages on the Ferris wheel have two people in them, **and**</u>
          <u>one carriage on the Ferris wheel has three people in it.</u>

          or <u>Three of the carriages on the Ferris wheel have two people in them, **but**</u>
          <u>one carriage on the Ferris wheel has three people in it.</u>

2. (a)   The two people are at the same level as the bird.
    (b)   They are feeding the bird.

    _____

3. (a)   The people in line are being patient.
    (b)   They may have to wait longer because the Ferris wheel is crowded.

    _____

4. (a)   The man has a flower in his hand.
    (b)   He wants to give the flower to the girl.

    _____

5. (a)   The girl is standing next to the Ferris wheel.
    (b)   She doesn't want to ride it, because she wants the boy to give her the flower.

    _____

    _____

6. (a)   I am afraid.
    (b)   I will be brave.

    _____

7. (a)   Hold on tight.
    (b)   We'll be down soon.

    _____

8. (a)   I should not have gone on this ride.
    (b)   I was challenged by Sue to do it.

    _____

9. (a)   Don't get too close to the fire-breathing man.
    (b)   The fire is spreading.

    _____

    _____

10. (c)   The kids have to move.
    (d)   The fire truck is coming.

    _____

11. (a)   The man is stuck on the coaster loop.
    (b)   The firemen will have to rescue him.

    _____

12. (c)   The man should not have climbed on top of the roller coaster.
    (d)   He must be drunk.

    _____

13. (a)   The man sells popcorn.
    (b)   The man sells cotton candy.

    _____

14. (c)   The popcorn is delicious.
    (d)   The popcorn costs too much.

    _____

15. (a)   The pig is running around freely.
    (b)   It should be on a leash.

    _____

    _____

16. (c)   The man is the pig's master.
    (d)   He should put his pig on a leash.

    _____

    _____

17. (a)   The fire truck is making a lot of noise.
    (b)   I am happy it is here because there is a fire.

    _____

    _____

16—Riding and Feeding Elephants in Ayuttyaha

Verb Tenses

This exercise tests student's knowledge of **verb tenses**.

Some verbs in this lesson are in the	**past**	tense.
Other verbs are to be used in the	**present**	tense.

Some of the verbs are	**regular**	verbs.
Other verbs are	**irregular**	verbs.

(1)   Regular Verbs

Add **ed** to the end of the verb to form the **past tense**.

Examples:	Present Tense	Past Tense
	ask	asked
	move	moved

For some verbs that **end** in **y**, change the **y** to **i**, then add **ed** at the end of the verb to form the past tense.

Examples:	Present Tense	Past Tense
	hurry	hurried
	marry	married

For other verbs that end in **y**, don't change the **y** to **i**. Leave the verb ending **as is** and add **ed** to the end of the verb to form the past tense.

Examples:	Present Tense	Past Tense
	stay	stayed
	sway	swayed

(2)   Irregular Verbs

There are no set rules for forming the past tense of an irregular verb. Look up the past tense of irregular verbs in verb tables.

Irregular verbs <u>used in this lesson</u>:

be	buy	feed	get	go	has
make	ride	run	see	tell	think
thrust					

Regular verbs <u>used in this lesson</u>:

ask	chain	control	decide	enjoy	excite
fulfill	gobble	love	pet	raise	
remember	return	sway	stamp	startle	visit

Irregular Verbs

Past	Present	Future
was were	be	be
bought	buy	buy
fed	feed	feed
got	get	get
went	go	go
had	has	have
made	make	make
rode	ride	ride
ran	run	run
saw	see	see
told	tell	tell
thought	think	think
thrust	thrust	thrust

See appendix D for lists of irregular verbs.

Regular Verbs

Past	Present	Future
asked	ask	ask
chained	chain	chain
controlled	control	control
decided	decide	decide

enjoyed	enjoy	enjoy
excited	excite	excite
fulfilled	fulfill	fulfill
gobbled	gobble	gobble
loved	love	love
petted	pet	pet
raised	raise	raise
remembered	remember	remember
returned	return	return
swayed	sway	sway
stamped	stamp	stamp
startled	startle	startle
visited	visit	visit

Practice Exercise: Place the verbs in the blanks according to the correct verb tense.

1. **keep, kept**
   (a) _____ your dog in the yard.
   (b) I _____ my dog in the yard

2. **accept, accepted**
   (a) I _____ his apology after the accident.
   (b) Please _____ my apology for the accident.

3. **ride, rode**
   (a) Pun wants to _____ the elephant.
   (b) Pun _____ the elephant yesterday.

4. **go, went**
   (a) I _____ to the game yesterday.
   (b) I won't _____ to the game today.

5. **return, returned**
   (a) Prim _____ the book.
   (b) Prim will _____ the book later.

6. **don't, didn't**
   (a) I _____ say that.
   (b) I _____ say things like that.

7. **carry, carried**
   (a) Krit already _____ the books.
   (b) Krit will _____ the books.

8. **drank, drink**
   (a) Kanoon _____ the juice.
   (b) Kanoon will _____ the juice.

9. **has, have**
   (a) Suchera _____ a dog.
   (b) Suchera used to _____ a dog.

10. **sure, was sure** (a) Is Ploy _____ about that?
    (b) Ploy _____ about that.

11. **sleep, slept** (a) Fah already _____.
    (b) Fah will _____ soon.

12. **study, studied** (a) Haddis _____ hard for the final exam.
    (b) Haddis will _____ hard for the final exam.

Main Exercise: In the stories, change the tense of the verb. Some verbs are regular verbs, some are irregular verbs. The change will often be from the present tense to the past tense. For some of the irregular verbs, the present and past tenses are identical.

Thai Wat, Ayuttyaha

I often **(go)** _____ to Ayuttyaha on day trips in 2006, when I lived in Bangkok. Ayuttyaha **(is)** _____ one of Thailand's ancient capitals, and it **(has)** _____ many temples. I **(visit)** _____ Ayuttyaha often to see its temples, and on many of those visits, I **(see)** _____ people riding elephants. I therefore **(decide)** _____ to follow an elephant one time to see where it **(go)** _____.

On one of those trips, I **(fulfill)** _____ one of my dreams: I **(ride)** _____ an elephant! I don't **(remember)** _____ the name of the elephant I rode on because I **(be)** _____ too excited. The elephant **(is)** _____ huge, and it **(have)** _____ a baby elephant **(attach)** _____ to it by a chain. I was **(tell)** _____ this was necessary, because if elephants **(hear)** _____ a loud noise, then they may **(run)** _____ away, or they may (stampede) _____. When the baby is (chain) _____ to the bigger elephant, then the big elephant will not (run) _____. The baby is therefore (chain) _____ to the bigger elephant so that it will (be) _____ safer for the rider.

Riding an Elephant in Thailand

We (go) _____ to an elephant stable, where there (be) _____ many other elephants. I (see) _____ other people feeding the elephants in the stable, so I (ask) _____ if I could also feed the elephants. I was (tell) _____ where to buy food for the elephants, so I (go) _____ to this place and (buy) _____ a bunch of fruit and sugarcane. I then eagerly (go) _____ to the stable and found a big, cute elephant.

The elephant's name was Jamjali. He was really eager, so he (raise) _____ his trunk up in the air and (make) _____ a loud noise. I then (thrust) _____ some sugarcane in Jamjali's direction, and he (gobble) _____ it up like a big, hungry elephant would. Jamjali let me (pet) _____ him, and this was fun, so I went and (buy) _____ some more food for him.

When I (return) _____, Jamjali was with his friend Jumpy. I (buy) _____ a lot of food, so there was enough for both elephants. Jamjali and Jumpy let me pet them as I (feed) _____ them, so this was great fun. Both elephants (love) _____ the food, so I was able to (make) _____ instant friends with both of them.

All the elephants in the stable (be) _____ friendly and playful, especially when you were feeding them. The elephants also loved it when people would pet their trunk and the side of their head, so everyone (enjoy) _____ themselves at the elephant stable. After feeding the elephants, I (go) _____ to the front gate and (ask) _____ if I could ride an elephant. I was (tell) _____ that anyone could (ride) _____ an elephant. When I was (tell) _____ the price, I (think) _____ it was a very good deal.

When I **(get)** _____ on top of the elephant, I was very excited. I also noticed that a baby elephant was **(chain)** _____ to the big elephant I was on. I was **(tell)** _____ this was done to stop the big elephant from running away during the ride. Elephants can be easily **(startle)** _____ when they hear loud noises, such as the sound of the horn of a car, so they sometimes **(stampede)** _____ when this happens. This can be very dangerous for the rider, because he or she can **(fall)** _____ off if the elephant runs.

A man **(rode)** _____ in front of me and he did a good job of controlling the elephant. As I **(ride)** _____ the elephant, I could **(feel)** _____ how powerful it **(be)** _____. I easily **(sway)** _____ back and forth a lot on the ride. It was the best ride I ever **(have)** _____, though.

17—Shaman Healers

Prepositions

A **preposition** is a word that shows a relationship between nouns, pronouns, and other words in a sentence.

Prepositions are *always* found in prepositional phrases.

Examples:

Sentence			Prepositional Phrase	
(1) The pie is	**on**	the table.	on	the table
(2) She is	**at**	school.	at	school
(3) He lives	**in**	a house.	in	a house

repositional phrases always: (a)   start with a preposition and

                                   (b)   end with a noun or pronoun.

The <u>first noun</u> or <u>pronoun</u> after the preposition is the <u>object</u> of the <u>preposition</u>.

Prepositional Phrase		Object of the Preposition
(1) on	the table	table
(2) at	school	school
(3) in	a house	house

A prepositional phrase **must** contain the following:

    (a)   a preposition

    (b)   an object of the preposition

If these two requirements are **not** met, then the word is **not** a <u>preposition</u>.

Examples:

Sentence	Prepositional Phrase
(1) The child ran down the stairs.	down the stairs

In sentence (1), **down** is in a prepositional phrase; therefore, it is a preposition.

(2) The teacher said, "The test is over. Please put your pencils down."

In sentence (2), **down** <u>is not</u> in a prepositional phrase; therefore, it <u>is not</u> a preposition. Down is used as an adverb in sentence (2).

List of Prepositions

The prepositions **of, to,** and **in** are among the ten most frequently used words in English. This is a short list of seventy of the more common prepositions.

- about   above   across   after   at   as
- against   along   amid   among   around
- before   behind   below   beneath   beside
- between   beyond   but   by
- concerning   considering
- despite   down   during
- except   excepting   excluding
- following   for   from
- inside   into   in
- like
- minus
- near   nearby
- off   on   onto   opposite   outside   over
- past   per   plus
- regarding   round
- save   since
- than   through   to   toward
- under   unlike   until   underneath   up   upon
- versus   via
- with   within   without

1. Review appendix B.
2. Review and understand the list of vocabulary used in the story.

Nouns

<u>elder</u>	- an older person who is respected or who is higher in rank
<u>stress</u>	- nervousness, anxiety, emotional tension
<u>acknowledgment</u>	- to be recognized
	- to be understood and to receive recognition
<u>public</u>	- all the people
	- everyone

<u>reputation</u>	- a person's character
	- the way a person is respected or thought of by others
<u>ritual</u>	- a certain method or way that a group performs something
	- a ceremony for a religious or cultural group
<u>sorcerer</u>	- wizard, magician, conjurer
<u>tribe</u>	- a group or class of people with common beliefs or customs

Adjectives

<u>enhanced</u>	- increased, heightened, bigger, larger
<u>modernized</u>	- to change from old to the new

Phrases with Adjectives and Nouns

<u>public</u> <u>acknowledgment</u>	- to be recognized or to be understood by the public
	- to be appreciated by the public
<u>spiritual healer</u>	- a type of doctor
	- this doctor does not use medicine to heal but instead uses spiritual methods
<u>spiritual healing</u>	- to heal or cure a person with spiritual methods
<u>white magic</u>	- to control or to be able to foresee something

Verbs

<u>break</u>	- to destroy, to split into pieces
<u>cure</u>	- to make something or someone healthy
	- to fix or make something or someone better
<u>practice</u>	- to do a thing regularly
	- to do something as a habit
	- to perform an act over and over again
<u>recite</u>	- to say something from memory

Adverb

<u>enthusiastically</u>	- to do something with passion, a lot of emotion, or spirit

Main Exercise—Tribal Shamans, Spirit Doctors, and Sorcerers

Directions: Read this short story about tribal shamans and spiritual healers in Thailand. The difficult words for this story have been reviewed above.

Tribal shamans are spiritual healers for Thai tribes. They cure people who have not responded to modern medicine or modern doctors. Most shamans are women, and they learn <u>spiritual healing</u> by watching <u>elders</u> who <u>recite</u> the texts. The learning sessions can last hours, and there are usually no <u>breaks</u>. Spiritual healers receive a free meal when they cure a person.

More importantly, spiritual healers receive <u>public acknowledgment</u> of their skill and an <u>enhanced</u> <u>reputation</u>. After Thailand <u>modernized</u>, this increased people's <u>stress</u>, so the spiritual healers became important. Spirit doctors are different from Tribal shamans because they <u>practice white magic</u>.

<u>Sorcerers</u> are another type of healer. They are from non-Thai ethnic groups and usually live on the Thai border. Sorcerers also practice a type of black magic. Thais <u>enthusiastically</u> watch the <u>rituals</u>, but they also must sit still during the performance. Tribal shamans, spirit doctors, and sorcerers are therefore types of healers that many Thai people depend on for their healing.

Directions: Refer to the story to choose the correct preposition in the sentence:

1. Tribal shamans act **like / with** _____ spiritual healers for Thais.

2. Tribal shamans try to cure people who have not responded to the modern medicine that is practiced **as / by** _____ modern doctors.

3. Most shamans are women who learn **about / with** _____ spiritual healing by sitting **beside / up** _____ an elder, who recites the texts.

4. Learning sessions can last hours, **without / to** _____ a break.

5. Spiritual healers receive a free meal **for / in** _____ their services.

6. More important **for / about** _____ the spiritual healer, though, is the public acknowledgment of their skill and their enhanced reputation.

7. The modernization **of / by** _____ Thailand has increased the stress on Thais, which makes the spiritual healer's work more important.

8. White magic is practiced **by / on** _____ spirit doctors.

9. Sorcerers from non-Thai ethnic groups who live **along / by** _____ the border come **into / by** _____ Thailand to practice black magic.

10. Sorcerers use love potions **on / onto** _____ their followers.

11. Love potions are usually produced **from / by** _____ corpse chin oil.

12. When spirit doctors contact a spirit, the spirit speaks **through / with** _____ the doctor, to communicate **with / in** _____ relatives.

13. Spirit doctors wear leopard skin hats **on / in** _____ their heads.

14. Spirit doctors wear the robes **of / by** _____ traditional hermits.

15. Ritual defines a shaman's approach **of / with** _____ the spirit world.

16. Only experienced priests or spirit doctors know how to appease or properly deal **with / by** _____ angry spirits.

17. Thais enthusiastically join **in / with** _____ on rituals, but they must sit still during the performance **of / with** _____ the ritual.

Prepositions and Prepositional Phrases

In the sentences below, determine whether the **word in bold** is a <u>preposition</u> or an <u>adverb</u>. Explain your answer.

1. The Thai lady was healed **by** the tribal shaman.

<u>Answer:</u>   <u>**By** is in a prepositional phrase (by the tribal shaman). Therefore, it is a preposition.</u>

2. When the tribal shaman cured the lady, she was so excited that she could not sit **down.**

<u>Answer:</u>   <u>The word **down** is not in a prepositional phrase, so it is not a preposition. It is an adverb.</u>

3. Sorcerers live **along** the Thai border.

<u>Answer:</u>   _____

   _____

4. When the boys would not keep quiet during a healing session, the shaman told them to go **outside**.

<u>Answer:</u>   _____

   _____

5. The lady thought the love potion given to her **by** the sorcerer would help her husband, but it did not.

<u>Answer:</u>   _____

   _____

6. Spiritual healers are concerned **about** public acknowledgment of their skills.

<u>Answer:</u>   _____

   _____

7. Healing is what spiritual healers are concerned **with**.

Answer: _____

_____

8. After I saw a spiritual healer, my troubles were in the **past**.

Answer: _____

_____

9. Spiritual healing is very popular **in** Thailand.

Answer: _____

_____

10. Thais enthusiastically watch the rituals, but they also must sit still **during** the performance.

Answer: _____

_____

11. Tribal shamans are spiritual healers **for** Thai tribes.

Answer: _____

_____

18—The Thai Jungle

Action Verbs versus State of Being Verbs

Action Verbs

The most common function of a **verb**: it can produce or provide an **action**.

"Jane **ran** to school."   The verb **ran** tells the reader **what** Jane **did**.

These types of verbs are called **action verbs**.

State of Being Verbs

A **verb** can also express a **state of being**.

This implies they can also describe an **inactive condition**.

"It **is** hot today."
"The children **are** in school."   The verbs **is** and **are** tell the reader about **conditions** that are **inactive**.

Certain verbs can sometimes function as both action verbs and state of being verbs, depending on how they are used in a sentence.

Example: Taste used as an **action verb** and as a **state of being verb**

(1) I **tasted** Susan's lasagna, and it was fabulous.	**action verb**
(2) My lasagna **tastes** different.	**state of being verb**

Sentence 1: **Tasted** is an **action verb**. The word **tasted** explains what I did or what **action** I undertook.

Sentence 2: **Tastes** is a **state of being verb**. It indicates something about the **sense** of **taste**, **not** the **action** of tasting.

Example: Orbit used as an **action verb** and as a **state of being verb**

> (3) Numerous satellites **orbit** the earth.
>
> (4) Neptune **orbits** on its side.

Sentence 3:   **Orbit** functions as an **action verb.**
It tells the reader what the satellites **are doing.**
The satellites are **moving** or **going around** the earth.
It expresses an **action.**

Sentence 4:   **Orbit** functions as a **state of being verb.**
It indicates **something about** Neptune orbits, **not** the **action** of
the orbiting.
It expresses a **state of being**.

Practice Exercise: In this exercise, write sentences using the indicated verb. Write the verb as

(a)   an action verb

(b)   a state of being verb

1. **sleep**   (a) I **slept** last night.

        (b) My mother **sleeps** on her side.

2. **throw**   (a) _____

        (b) _____

3. **plan**   (a) _____

        (b) _____

4. **walk**   (a) _____

        (b) _____

5. **taste**   (a) _____

        (b) _____

Main Exercise: Indicate if the verbs below are action verbs (A) or state of being verbs (S).

1. <u>A</u>_____ The monkey **swung** from the trees.

2. <u>S</u>_____ This durian **tastes** horrible.

3. _____ The golden leaf on the temple **shone** brightly.

4. _____ The elephants **sprayed** water on us.

5. _____ The elephants **lay** down on their sides.

6. _____ Dolphins **are** playful animals.

7. _____ The Chao Lei, or people of the sea, **make** a living off fishing.

8. _____ Boys of the hill tribes **are** good trappers.

9. _____ Boys in hill tribes **learn** to be trappers when they are young.

10. _____ Some Thai hill tribes eat insects, because the body of the insect **contains** keratin, which provides protein for the tribes.

11. _____ At Lopburi, monkeys **swarm** over the temples when people put food in the temples for the monkeys on a special day.

12. _____ Water buffalo **are** huge creatures.

13. _____ Water buffalo never **lie** on their sides.

14. _____ Queen Chamadevi **was** a popular queen in the seventh century.

15. _____ Thais **recreate** the splendor of Queen Chamadevi's court during a special festival in winter.

16. _____ Northern hill tribes **wear** bright costumes during New Year's.

17. _____ The women's colorful costumes **shine** brightly.

18. _____ The Padaung women of the Mae Hong Son tribe **wear** neck rings.

19. _____ Yao women of the northern tribes **design** embroidered trousers.

20. _____ The rice spirit **is** a well-respected spirit.

19—Thailand and Its People

Apostrophes: Possessive, Is, One and More Than One

An apostrophe can signify one of two things:

Possession: (1)   That is Tanya**'s** car.

Is: (2)   **That's** my dog.
                     That is my dog.

Exercise A: Choose whether the apostrophe signifies **possession** or **is**.

	Phrase	**Choice**	
Example 1:	Jim's hungry	possessive	is
Correct Answer:	**is**	Jim **is** hungry.	
So you would circle or highlight **is**:		possessive	**is**
Example 2:	Jim's toy	possessive	is
Correct Answer:	**possession**	the toy **belongs** to Jim	
So circle or highlight **possessive**:		**possessive**	is

Exercise A: Circle or highlight **possession** or **is** for the sentences below.

1.	The **dugong's** floating	possession	**is**
2.	The **dolphin's** fin	possession	is
3.	The **dolphin's** swimming	possession	is
4.	King **Bhumibol's** throne	possession	is
5.	The **turtle's** shell	possession	is
6.	The **turtle's** not moving	possession	is
7.	The **jungle's** trees	possession	is

8.	**Jumpy's** running	possession	is
9.	**Ayuttyaha's** temples	possession	is
10.	The **paraglider's** flying	possession	is
11.	The **tiger's** tale	possession	is
12.	The **turtle's** hunting for food	possession	is
13.	The **monkey's** climbing	possession	is
14.	The **elephant's** trunk	possession	is
15.	The **girl's** snorkeling	possession	is

Exercise B: In the following sentences, decide if there is **1** or **more than 1**.

If there is only one, then the **apostrophe** is placed in between the word and **s**.
If there is more than one, then the **apostrophe** is placed after the **s**.

Examples:	The plantation's crops	<u>**one**</u>	more than one
	The plantations' crops	one	<u>**more than one**</u>

1.	The **dolphin's** nose	<u>**1**</u>	more than 1
2.	The **dolphins'** food	1	more than 1
3.	The **hot spring's** jets	1	more than 1
4.	The **monks'** robes	1	more than 1
5.	**Bangkok's** river	1	more than 1
6.	**Bangkok's** royal palace	1	more than 1
7.	The **durians'** aroma	1	more than 1
8.	The **rowers'** oars	1	more than 1
9.	The coral **reef's** treasures	1	more than 1
10.	The **wats'** burial grounds	1	more than 1
11.	**Phuket's** nightlife	1	more than 1

12. Ko **Chang's** beauty   1   more than 1

13. The **princes'** jewelry   1   more than 1

14. The **elephant's** trunk   1   more than 1

15. The **elephants'** trunks   1   more than 1

110—Thailand's Floating Market

Since and For Many and Much

Since and **for** can be used to say **how long** something **has been happening**.

Since: since + the **start** of the **period**
For: for + a **period of time**

Since	For
I've been living in Trat **since** 1995.	I've been living in Trat **for** twenty years.
Bangkok has been Thailand's capital **since** 1757.	Bangkok has been Thailand's capital **for** more than 250 years.
I haven't had a coconut drink **since** Monday.	I haven't had a coconut drink **for** five days.
I think we should leave. We've been waiting **since** 1:00 p.m.	I think we should leave. We've been waiting **for** an hour.

It is possible to **leave out for** in some sentences, but do **not leave out for** in **negative sentences**.

1.   (a)   I have lived in Chang Mai **for** ten years.   **Correct**
      (b)   I have lived in Chang Mai ten years.   **Correct**

2.   (a)   I haven't been to Bangkok **for** five years.   **Correct**
      (b)   I haven't been to Bangkok five years.   **Incorrect xxx**

Practice Exercise One: Write **for** or **since** in the spaces.

1. It's been raining _____ yesterday.

2. Poon's been on holiday _____ four days.

3. Poon's been on holiday _____ Friday.

4. I haven't watched a game _____ our team was last in the playoffs.

5. I haven't been to watch a hockey game _____ two years.

6. I haven't been on a holiday _____ five years.

7. Achita's been absent _____ last Friday.

8. It's been cloudy _____ one hour.

9. It's been cloudy _____ 1:00 p.m.

10. I haven't eaten fish _____ one week.

Count and Non-Count Nons
Many, Much, A Lot, A Little, and A Few

Non-count Nouns

Noncount nouns are nouns that **cannot** be counted.

Use **much**, **a lot,** and **a little** for noncount nouns.

These are nouns like **blood**, **pollution**, and **water** that cannot be counted.

When using **noncount nouns:**   **Plurals** are **not** allowed.
                                                        Numbers are **not** used.

All the following six sentences are incorrect.

Plurals are **not** allowed: Numbers are **not** used:
Lots of **bloods** was on the ground.   I have **one blood** in my body.
The **pollutions** are hurting my eyes.   There is **one pollution** in the sky today.
                                               There is **a few pollution** in the sky today.
There is one **waters** in the sea.   I'd like to have **one water**.

All six sentences above are **incorrect**. It is **Incorrect** to use numbers in these sentences.

The following sentences demonstrate **correct ways** to use **noncount nouns**:

- How **much** money do you have?   I have **a lot** of money.
- Do you have **a lot** of pain?   No, I don't have **much** pain.
- How **much** rain will there be?   There will be **a little** rain.

A Short List of Some Noncount Nouns:

acid, air, blood, beef, construction, danger, drought, fluid, food, fruit, fun, gas, ice cream, ice tea, juice, knowledge, luck, money, noise, oil, paper, patience, people, pollution, pork, rain, rice, smog, soup, sun, sunscreen, water, wind, work

---

Sample sentences using **Non-count Nouns**

How **much** work did you do?

He lost **a lot** of blood.

There is **a lot** of construction in the city now.

How **much** gas do we need to fill the tank?

There's only **a litte** <u>rain</u>, we can still play soccer.

Teachers must have **a lot** of patience.

There's too **much** <u>smog</u> in the air today.

Note: in the above sentences, the nouns can **never be plurals**. Also, the word **many** can never be used with non-count nouns.

Practice Exercise Two: Make five sentences with the noncount nouns above. First, ask a question using **much.** Then answer the question with either **a little** or **a lot**.

<u>Example:</u>

How **much** soup did you eat?   I ate **a lot** of soup.

How **much** gas is there in the car?   There's only **a little** gas in the car.

1. _____

2. _____

3. _____

4. _____

5. _____

<u>**Count Nouns**</u>

Count nouns are nouns that **can** be counted.

Use **many** and **a few** for count nouns. **A little** cannot be used with count nouns.

These are nouns like **apples**, **cars**, and **chairs** that can be counted.

Plurals are allowed when using count nouns.

When using **count nouns**:   **Plurals are** allowed.
   Numbers can be used.

<u>Plurals **are** allowed:</u>   <u>Numbers **can be** used:</u>

There are **lots of apples** on the tree.   I ate **one apple**.   I ate **five apples**.

The **chairs** are beautiful.   I bought **four chairs**.

There are **many dogs** in the park.   Samantha has **two dogs**.

A Short List of Some Count Nouns:

apple, arm, bike, boat, book, bowl, boy, car, carrot, century, cloud, coat, dress, elephant, fork, girl, grape, house, kilometer, lamp, mango, map, market, pen, people, pool, river, road, shirt, spoon, table, tree, word, zebra

Practice Exercise Three: Make five sentences with the count nouns above. First, ask a question using **many.** Then answer the question using **a number, a little** or **a lot.**

<u>Example:</u>
How **many clouds** are in the sky?   There are only **five clouds**.
How **many spoons** do we need for the party?   We need **ten spoons**.

1. _____

2. _____

3. _____

4. _____

5. _____

Practice Exercise Four — Many and Much

For the following ten sentences, check to see whether the noun is **count** or **non-count**.
Then in the blanks, use the words: **a few**   for   **count** nouns
                                      a little   for   **noncount** nouns

Example: How **much luck** did you have in Vegas?
Answer: **Luck** is a **non-count noun**. So only **a few** or **a litle** can be used in the answer. A **number** cannot be used in the answer.
Answer: I only had _____a little_____ **luck** in Vegas this time.

1. How **many apples** did you buy?
   I bought _____ **apples**.
2. The library only has _____ Physics **books**.
3. We saw _____ **otters** by the beach today.
4. How **much pollution** is there in Bangkok?
   There's only _____ **pollution** in Bangkok.
5. I only have _____ **time** to spare.

6. How **many** Chinese **words** do you know?
   I only know _____ Chinese **words**.
7. There was only _____ **traffic** today, so I arrived early.
8. Tammy only wants _____ **soup**.
9. I only have _____ **paper** left.
10. Kara only caught _____ **balls** today. She dropped so many of the balls that came to her.

Practice Exercise Five: Choose the correct word in the following sentences. The revelant nouns in each sentence are underlined.

1.   **for**   **since**

   (a) Floating markets have existed in Thailand _____ the **nineteenth century**.
   (b) Floating markets have existed in Thailand _____ **hundreds of years**.

2.   **many**   **much**

   (a) There were lots of canals in Bangkok in the nineteenth century, so Bangkok had _____ more **floating markets** then.

   (b) When I went to Damnoen Saduak Floating Market in 2006, there was so _____ **fruit** for sale.

3.   **many**   **much**

   (a) It doesn't cost _____ **money** to ride a boat at the floating markets.
   (b) How _____ **boats** do you see on the river?

4.   **many**   **a lot**

   (a) Bangkok has _____ **rivers**, so in the 1800s, the city was known as the Venice of the East.

   (b) The women operating the boats at the markets have _____ of **knowledge** on how to operate their boats on the fast-flowing rivers.

5.   **a lot**   **one-hundred**

   (a) Damnoen Saduak Floating Market has _____ of **people**.
   (b) Damnoen Saduak is _____ **kilometers** from Bangkok.

6.   **a little**   **seven**

   (a)   We will buy _____ **juice** at Amphawa Floating Market.
   (b)   I bought _____ **mangoes** at Amphawa Floating Market.

7.   **for**   **since**

   (a)   Let's go home, I've been here _____ **9:00AM**.
   (b)   We stayed at the floating market _____ **four hours**.

8.   **for**   **since**

   (a)   Women boat operators are in the sun _____ many **hours**.
   (b)   Ayutthyaha's market has been operating _____ **the year 1350**.

9.   **many**   **much**

   (a)   I didn't drink _____ **water** at the market, because I ate a lot of fruit.
   (b)   The women operating the boats at the markets have worn traditional indigo shirts and straw hats for _____ **centuries**.

10.   **five**   **much**

   (a)   There are _____ **floating markets** close to Bangkok.
   (b)   At 12 noon, there was too _____ **noise** at the market, because it become very crowded with people and boats.

Main Exercise: Choose the correct word in the parentheses in the story.

The Menan Chao Praya Basin covers **(many / much)** _____ of the areas near Bangkok. Bangkok itself lies on the Chao Praya River. **(For / Since)** _____ many centuries before today, people traveled in boats along the rivers in the basin, so there were **(many / much)** _____ boats that traveled these waters a century ago. Since water travel was the main form of transportation, floating markets were very common. Floating markets have therefore existed in Thailand _____ **(for / since)** a long time. There were **(many / much)** _____ canals in Bangkok in the nineteenth century, so Bangkok had **(many / much)** _____ more canals and floating markets then.

   Damnoen Saduak, which is 110 kilometers north of Bangkok, is a flourishing Thai floating market. The market is popular with Thais but attracts **(many / much)** _____ tourists as well. There are **(many / much)** _____ things for sale at the market, but when I last went there, I bought **(a lot of/ much)** _____ fruit. The prices are low, so I only spent **(a little / a few)** _____ money. Amphawa Floating Market, another floating market near Bangkok, is less crowded.

   The history of the canal systems and travel by boat along canals is interesting. In premodern days, **(many / much)** _____ of the area around Bangkok was full of swamps. Thais then cleared **(a lot / a few)** _____ of this land for rice cultivation. People still had to travel through these rice fields, so **(many / much)** _____ canals were built. The canals are called *klong* in Thai. Water was channeled through these canals, so boat travel increased along the canals. Then, in the twentieth century, the introduction of the automobile spelled the end for **(many / much)** _____ canals in Thailand. **(Many / Much)** _____ Thai farmers still own boats, though, because **(many / much)** _____ of the vast klong system is still in place outside Bangkok.

Bangkok was known as the Venice of the East **(for / since)** _____ much of the nineteenth century, but this is no longer the case. **(Many / Much)** _____ klongs in Bangkok have been paved over to make way for cars. There are only **(a few / a little)** _____ canals in Bangkok now. It is still easy to take a trip to Damnoen Saduak Floating Market though, as it is near to Bangkok. A trip there only costs **(a few / a little)** _____ money, and the trip is well worth it. At the market, you will notice that the people operating the boats are older ladies. It doesn't cost **(many / much)** _____ money to hire a boat. It's an exciting thing to do, because when traveling on the canal, you visit the various markets that are tightly and neatly arranged along the riverbank.

The women operating the boats at the markets still wear the traditional indigo shirt and straw hat. I also noticed that they wear makeup but not too **(many / much)** _____ of it. I was surprised at how healthy these women were, because they are senior citizens, but still, they paddle their boats along the river. They operate them with ease, so it only takes **(a few / a little)** _____ effort. The women have been operating these boats **(for / since)** _____ the last century, so they are good at it. The women are definitely one of the things that make the floating markets fun places to visit.

I11—Dimensions
Thai Beaches and Wats

The following words can express **dimensions**:

Nouns:	length	width	height	depth	thickness
Adjectives:	long	wide	high	deep	thick

Comparing words that express dimensions:

Adjectives	Nouns
Long The shark **was** five meters **long**.	**Length** The shark **had** a **length** of five meters.
Wide The elephant **was** so **wide** it couldn't fit in the door.	**Width** The elephant's **width was** so great it couldn't fit in the door.
High Bangkok's tallest building **is** four hundred meters **high**.	**Height** Bangkok's tallest building **has** a **height** of four hundred meters.
Deep It doesn't matter how **deep** the ocean **is**; a person can still see to the bottom because Kata Beach's water is so clear.	**Depth** It doesn't matter **what** the **depth** of the ocean **is**; a person can still see to the bottom of Kata Beach's water because it is so clear.
Thick The dolphin's fin **is** 20 cm **thick**.	**Thickness** The dolphin's fin **has** a **thickness** of 20 cm.

Practice Exercise: Make a sentence from the information given.

1. Shoulder   Asian elephant   width   three meters
   The <u>shoulder</u> **width** of an <u>Asian elephant</u> can be up to <u>three meters.</u>

2. Surfboard   long   two meters

3. Clownfish can live waters   depth   hundreds of meters

_____

4. Dolphin can jump   high   two meters

_____

5. Tail of a whale   long   two meters

_____

6. Edges of an elephant's ears   thickness   a few centimeters

_____

7. Dugong's body   length   three meters

_____

8. A mermaid's tail can be   long   one meter

_____

9. A turtle's shell can be   wide   one meter

_____

10. Dolphins can swim in water   deep   many meters

_____

11. Coral reef   length   many kilometers

_____

12. A whale can blow water   height   many meters

_____

Exercise: Students will use the words that are given and make sentences out of them. One sentence will involve the use of an adjective, such as **thick**, and the other sentence will involve the use of a noun, such as **thickness**.

1. Cha Am Beach   long   length   forty kilometers

     (a) Cha Am's beach is forty kilometers **long**. _____

     (b)   Cha Am's beach has a **length** of forty kilometers _____

2. Reefs at Ko Phangang   deep   depth   twenty meters

   (a) _____

   (b) _____

3. Standing Buddha on Khao Takiab high   height   twenty meters

   (a) _____

   (b) _____

4. Shoulder width   Asian elephant   wide   width   three meters

   (a) _____

   (b) _____

5. Solid gold Buddha, Wat Chedi Sao   thick   thickness   3cm gold plate

   (a) _____

   (b) _____

6. Doi Suthep Mountain   high   height   1,676 meters

   (a) _____

   (b) _____

7. The Kinnaree statue's torso   long   length   several meters

   (a) _____

   (b) _____

8. Fine white sand beach at Ko Tao   long   length   2.5 kilometers

   (a) _____

   (b) _____

9. Wat Phra That Cho Hae's gilded Chedi   high   height   thirty-three meters

   (a) _____

   (b) _____

10. Emerald Buddha at Wat Phra Keo   wide   width   a few meters

    (a) _____

    (b) _____

11. Glass-bottom boat at Krabi Beach   thick   thickness   several centimeters

    (a) _____

    (b) _____

12. Paragliders at Hua Hin Beach can soar in the air   high   height   hundreds of meters

    (a) _____

    (b) _____

13. Chedi, Wat Thammamongkhon   high   height   ninety-five meters

    (a) _____

    (b) _____

I12—Joe in Phuket

Reflexive Pronouns

Reflexive Pronouns: Used when the subject and object refer to the same person.

	Pronoun	Reflexive Pronoun
I wrote a story about **myself**.	I	myself
We all wrote about **ourselves**.	We	ourselves

Rules: for **one person**, use the singular   self
            for **more than one person**, use the plural   selves

Reflexi Pronouns

Singular	Plural
myself	ourselves
yourself	yourselves
himself	themselves
herself	
itself	

Practice Exercise: Match the words in column A with the words in column B.

A		B
1. elephants	_____	(a) myself
2. my aunt	_____	(b) himself
3. you and your family	_____	(c) yourself
4. that boy	_____	(d) itself
5. the Jet Ski	_____	(e) themselves
6. my father	_____	(f) herself
7. me alone	_____	(g) ourselves
8. you alone	_____	(h) himself
9. me and my sister	_____	(i) yourselves

Practice Exercise: Place the reflexive pronouns into the correct sentences. The number in brackets after a word indicates how many times the word is used. (ie) (x2) indicates that the word is used twice in the story.

<u>Singular</u>   <u>Plural</u>
myself   (x1)   ourselves   (x1)
yourself   (x2)   yourselves   (x1)
himself   (x1)   themselves   (x1)
herself   (x2)
itself   (x1)

1. I could dress _____ when I was two years old.

2. Kanoon did her homework all by _____.

3. The teacher told the class, "I have already shown you how to do the lesson. Now you can finish the exercises by _____."

4. Prim learned how to water-ski all by _____.

5. The elephants can use their trunks and the water in the pond to wash _____.

6. The teacher also told the student, "You must turn off your computer before you leave. The computer will not turn _____ off."

7. Peera's father is a very versatile man. He rebuilt and redecorated their house all by _____.

8. When I asked my mother to wash my clothes, she told me, "You can wash your clothes by _____."

9. We drew some beautiful drawings when the teacher was called by the principal. We all knew we could work well by _____.

10. All children should learn how to wash _____ and brush their teeth by _____ before they start school.

11. Every man should learn to cook for _____.

12. The teacher told Kanoon, "You should learn how to use the computer all by _____."

Practice Exercise: Put the following words into the correct blanks in the essay.

myself (x2)	yourself (x2)	himself (x3)	herself (x2)
itself (x2)	ourselves (x1)	yourself (x1)	themselves (x5)

Joe went to Phuket by **(1)** _____ last weekend. Everyone else was sick, so they all stayed in Bangkok. Before Joe left, his father told the rest of the family, "I know you all want to go to Phuket, but you're all sick. You'd all better take care of **(2)** _____ so that we can all go together to Phuket next month."

After Joe returned, he told everyone about his trip to Phuket. He told them how he took lessons to operate a Jet Ski and then how he rented one and then drove it by **(3)** _____ on the ocean. Joe then talked about a good experience he had at the Jet Ski rental place. Joe met a girl there, and she was alone and by **(4)** _____, so she and Joe went Jet Skiing together. Joe explained how easy it was operate the Jet Ski, because it practically drives **(5)** _____. All you have to do is steer it a little bit, and it glides smoothly over the water.

After Jet Skiing, Joe and Pam, his new friend, watched the elephants play. The elephants could wash **(6)** _____, because they'd suck in water with their trunks and then spray it all over **(7)** _____. Pam actually tried to talk with an elephant, and this is what she said: "You are so clever. You can wash **(8)** _____, just like I can. So you are very clever." Joe noticed how the elephants were looking strangely at Pam, so he thought, *This is what they are thinking to* **(9)** _____: *Pam is crazy!*. Even though Joe was thinking to **(10)** _____ and not speaking out loud, Pam seemed to know what he was thinking, because she said, "I know what you're thinking. You're thinking to **(11)** _____. I suspect you think I'm crazy."

Pam and Joe had a good laugh at that, and then, surprisingly, it seemed that the elephants started laughing to **(12)** _____, so Pam and Joe concluded that elephants were indeed very intelligent. Pam then said, "I often laugh at **(13)** _____, because I sometimes do strange things, but if I don't laugh, then I might get too stressed out. My job is very hectic, so my coworkers agree that we have to laugh at **(14)** _____ at times to release the tension.

Joe and Pam then went to a restaurant. There was no one else there, so they had the whole place to **(15)** _____. Joe felt lucky because even though his family was not with him, he had met a fine lady. Pam was actually thinking the same thing to **(16)** _____, because her family had stayed behind in Bangkok as well, as they too were sick. Outside the restaurant, they saw a man with a monkey. The man was an organ grinder, but he did not have to operate the organ, because it ran by **(17)** _____. Joe had a wonderful time, so he said to Pam, "Next time I come to Phuket, I will not be coming by **(18)** _____. I will bring my family so you can meet them. Pam promised Joe the same thing, so they said goodbye and promised to meet again in Phuket very soon.

113—Thai Customs

Adjectives and Adverbs

Adjective: **describes** a noun or a pronoun.

Adverb: **modifies** a verb.

Adverbs and **adjectives** function in similar manners, but there are differences.

Adjectives: – qualify nouns and pronouns
   – nearly always appear before a noun or pronoun
   – offer degrees of comparison
   – have degrees of importance
      (They are ordered in terms of importance when
      describing a noun or a pronoun.)
   – can be accompanied by single words and phrases, called **premodifiers**, that
      intensify the degree of an adjective
         Example: This banana is **much more** <u>delicious</u> than the one I had this
         morning.

An **adjective** answers one of the following questions: **which one, what kind, how many.**

1.   <u>Which</u>   animal?   The <u>biggest</u> animal.
2.   <u>What kind</u>   of animal?   A <u>four-footed</u> animal.
3.   <u>How many</u>   animals?   <u>All</u> the animals in the zoo.

Adverbs: – modify verbs
   – can appear anywhere in a sentence
   – offer degrees of comparison
   – can be accompanied by single words and phrases, called **premodifiers**, that
      intensify the degree of an adverb.
         <u>Example</u>: I drove **a lot more** <u>carefully</u> after it rained.

Note: An adverb can often be derived from an adjective. Add **ly** to the end of the adjective to
make an adverb.

<u>Examples</u>:

Adjective	Adverb
beautiful	beautifully
calm	calmly

quick	quickly
powerful	powerfully

Practice Exercise—Animals, Sea Life, and Thai Beaches

Directions: Choose whether the **adverb** or **adjective** better fits in the sentence.

1. The elephant is a **powerful / powerfully** _____**powerful**_____ animal.

2. The elephant is a **powerful / powerfully** _____ built animal.

3. A dugong is a rare, **enchanting / enchantingly** _____ sea animal.

4. The dolphin is swimming **quick / quickly** _____.

5. The flying squirrel glided **graceful / gracefully** _____ through the air.

6. The big-eyed loris walked **slow / slowly** _____ through the bushes.

7. The gecko clung **strong / strongly** _____ to the wall.

8. The gecko had a **strong / strongly** _____ grip.

9. When I went to Krabi, I explored the beautiful fish when I went scuba diving in the **calm / calmly** _____ waters.

10. The boat **calm / calmly** _____ floated through Krabi's waters.

11. The big-eyed loris walked **slow / slowly** _____ through the bushes.

12. Clownfish are colored **brightly / bright** _____, and this helps them avoid predators because they can blend in with the corals.

13. Monkeys can play, just like human children do, so this provides **great / greatly** _____ entertainment for the people that watch them.

14. **Intensive / Intensely** _____ logging has destroyed much of the Thai elephant's natural habitat.

15. In previous times, Thai elephants were **ideal / ideally** _____ suited for moving and hauling logs deep in the forest.

Main Exercise—Thai Customs: Choose the correct **adjective** or **adverb**.

1. The Thai wat was **beautiful/beautifully** _____**beautifully**_____ decorated.

2. The Buddha statue was **amazing / amazingly** _____ huge.

3. The Thai performer wore **beautiful / beautifully** _____ clothes.

4. Thais believe the **royal / royally** _____ white elephant is sacred.

5. When a white elephant was brought to live in the palace, it was **royal / royally** _____ treated.

6. Mlarbi women swing **graceful / gracefully** _____ from ropes during their New Year's celebration.

7. There are no lions in Thailand, so Thais created very **stylish / stylishly** _____ portraits of the lion to be symbols of the monarchy.

8. Thais also created heavenly half beasts to serve as **appealing / appealingly** _____ depicted religious or mythical symbols.

9. Thais make great efforts to preserve their **ancient / anciently** _____ customs.

10. Buddhism is **deep / deeply** _____ embedded in Thailand.

11. In traditional Southern Thai theatre, pieces of buffalo hide are stretched **tight / tightly** _____ across pieces of wood to make puppets.

12. Monks roam Bangkok's streets and live **entire / entirely** _____ off donations that Thai people give them.

13. Thais mark the rainy season festivals by giving extra **generous / generously** _____ to monks in the rainy season.

14. At a mid-April's Bun Bang Fai festival at Isan, people fire **powerful / powerfully** _____ rockets at heaven to induce rain.

15. Festivals such as these in Isan are held so as to encourage the gods in heaven to make it rain **heavy / heavily** _____.

16. In the Flower Festival in Chang Mai, local women wear **beautiful / beautifully** _____ crafted clothes and headdresses.

17. Loi Krathong is the most **enchanting / enchantingly** _____ Thai festival, because people parade to the river with beautiful wicker lamps, and then place them **graceful / gracefully** _____ in the water.

18. Loi Krathong was **original / originally** _____ celebrated in Sukhothai.

19. Thai women put their hair up in the **traditional / traditionally** _____ way for Loi Krathong.

20. Thai women **tradition / traditionally** _____ put their hair up for Loi Krathong.

21. At Phuket's vegetarian festival, men run **quick / quickly** _____over hot coals.

22. In the ancient Thai capital of Ayuttyaha, statues, wats, and Buddha images sit **graceful / gracefully** _____ amongst the ruins.

23. Each Thai village has a **grand / grandly** _____ wat.

24. Thai monks live **virtuous / virtuously** _____ lives.

25. Thai monks live **virtuous / virtuously** _____ amongst the Thai people.

Main Exercise: Choose **ten** of the **words** from numbers 1–25 above and **write** your own sentences with these words. You can add extra words that are not shown in the sentences above.

Example: 4. adverb: <u>royally</u>   extra word: <u>lavish</u>

I was treated **<u>royally</u>** by my Thai friends when they took me out and treated me to a **lavish** dinner.

I14—Thai Water Sports and Activities

Modal Verbs

Modals verbs are helping verbs that support the main verb. They add extra information not given by the main verb.

Modal verbs <u>express the following conditions</u>:

assistance	necessity	lack of necessity	ability	inability
expectation	willingness	permission	advice	possibility
prohibition	suggestions	conclusions	logic	

Condition	Modal Verbs
ability	can, could
inability	cannot
assistance	would you, could you, will you, can you
advice	should, ought to, had better, shouldn't
conclusions	can, might, must have, must not
logical	must be, must have
necessity	have to, have got to, has to, had to, has got to, must
lack of necessity	do not have to
permission	can, could, may, might, shall
possibility	may, might, could
prohibition	must not
suggestions	should, shouldn't

Examples:

<u>Simple Sentence</u>	<u>Sentence with a Modal Verb Added to It</u>
Children go to school.	Children **must** go to school until grade twelve.
I eat apples.	I **should** eat apples instead of chips.

The modals **must** and **should** add extra meaning to the sentences. They support the main verb and do something the main verb cannot do.

Modal verbs **do not** use an **s** for third person plural:

Not Allowed: They musts have a coffee break.   XXX
                They shoulds eat lunch now.   XXX

Sample sentences with some modal verbs:

Krit	**can**	**speak** Spanish.	Ability
I	**must**	study for tomorrow's test.	Necessity
You	**should**	eat more vegetables.	Advice / Suggestion
Prang	**couldn't**	go out last night.	Permission (Past)

The following is a list of sample sentences for modal verbs:

can
- ability — He can speak Chinese.
- permission — Can I go home now?
- future permission — Can I go out dancing tonight?
- theoretical possibility — We can get to Mars one day, but when will that day come?

could
- ability in the past — I could dance better when I was younger.
- past permission — I couldn't use Mom's car yesterday.
- future permission — Could I use your car tonight?
- present possibility — We could just sit here and talk if you want.
- willingness — I could offer some help, if you'd like.

do
- express negatives — I don't eat wasabi.
- ask questions — Do you eat wasabi?
- express similarities — Tiger likes baseball, and so do I.
- express differences — Tiger likes wasabi, but I don't.
- adding emphasis — He does eat wasabi.

may
- permission — May I get a drink of water?
- possibility — Ms. Krump may be my teacher next year.

might (past tense of may)
- permission — If I finish my dinner, might I watch TV?
- possibility — It might rain tonight.

shall
- obligation — You shall clean your room each day.
- suggest an element of permission — Shall we go now?

will	intention	I will study tonight after dinner.
	willingness	I will sweep the floor.
	prediction	I think it will rain tonight.

would	intention	I will go home.
	willingness	Would you sweep the floor, please?
	prediction	I think it would be unfair to will rain tonight.
	insistence	You ate all the cake. You would do that.
	hypothetical	I would weigh more if I ate like you.
	sense of probability	I hear some noise. That would be the cat.
	characteristic activity	After school, she would always buy a malt.

used to   expresses an action that took place in the past
I used to study at Bangkok University.
expresses a sense that people are accustomed to something
I was worried when Pop moved out, but now I am used to it.

Practice: Place the correct modal in the blanks below. The condition is given.

1. Children _____ go to school until they are sixteen. (necessity)

2. Are we _____ to use a dictionary for this test?   (permission)

3. Give back my book or I _____ get angry!   (possibility)

4. You _____ be more careful with your money.   (suggestion)

5. You _____ be more careful with your money.   (necessity)

6. Books _____ be returned by midnight.   (suggestion)

7. Books _____ be returned by midnight.   (necessity)

8. Mom says you _____ clean your room.   (suggestion)

9. Mom says you _____ clean your room.   (necessity)

10. You _____ study hard when you go to college.   (advice)

Directions: In the following exercises, the modal verb is given. Find the condition.

11. He's never <u>had to</u> work hard.   <u>   Lack of necessity   </u>

12. I think you <u> should </u> try to eat less.   _____

13. ___Would you___ mind if I carry your bag for you? _____

14. ___Could___ you give my pen back later? _____

15. You ___must not___ drive if you drink. _____

16. What _should_ we do? We don't have any money. _____

17. I ___had to___ work late last night. _____

18. You _shouldn't_ eat pizza. You're on a diet. _____

Drinking

Jet-Skiing

Para-gliding

Water-Skiing

Sun Tanning

Dolphin Riding

Sailing

Surfing

Snorkeling

Main Exercise—Modals, Water Sports, and on the Beach in Thailand: Choose a modal verb to describe the picture. Then write the condition.

1. When paragliding, a person ___should___ wear a helmet.
    suggestion/advice

2. Surfers _____ be careful of sharks.
    _____

3. When suntanning, a person _____ wear sunscreen.
    _____

4. "_____ please tell me where the best beach
    is in Thailand?" _____

5. You _____ have prior experience to operate a Jet Ski. _____

6. Jet Ski riders _____ wear life jackets. _____

7. It _____ be difficult to learn how to surf. _____

8. _____ Prim water-ski? _____

9. People _____ feed the whales at the aquarium. _____

10. Jet Skiers _____ drive their Jet Skis close to people. _____

11. Professional surfers _____ be able to ride a huge wave. _____

12. Water-skiers_____ get too close to the boat. _____

13. Children _____ Jet Ski. _____

14. Elephants _____ Jet Ski or surf. _____

15. Children _____ be with their parents when swimming. _____

16. People _____ race each other on Jet Skis. _____

17. Water-skiers _____ come too close to shore. _____

18. A person _____ be older than nineteen to rent a boat. _____

19. Jet Skiers _____ hotdog too much on their Jet Skis. _____

20. Sailors _____ wear life jackets on their boats. _____

21. On hot days, you _____ drink a lot of fluids.

_____

22. People _____ ride dolphins.

_____

23. People _____ be kind to all marine life in the sea.

_____

A1—The Hindu Influence in Thailand

Adjective Clauses
Writing Descriptive Sentences

Sentences can be made more **descriptive** by changing the **adjective** into an **adjective clause**.

Clause: a structure with a subject and a verb. There are two kinds of clauses:

(1)   independent clause   (2)   dependent clause

Independent clauses are full sentences; **dependent clauses** are not.
Dependent clauses must be connected to **independent clauses**.
An **adjective clause** is a **dependent clause**.

Sentence (1): I met a kind man.   This a <u>full sentence.</u>
                                                          This is an <u>independent clause</u>.

Sentence (2): who is kind to everyone.   This is **not** a <u>full sentence.</u>
                                                          This is a <u>dependent clause.</u>

Example: Change the sentence into a <u>descriptive sentence</u> by changing the <u>adjective</u> into an <u>adjective clause</u>. Put the <u>noun</u> before the <u>adjective clause</u>.

<u>Simple sentence</u>:   (1) I met a kind man.   <u>adjective</u>:   kind
                                                                <u>noun</u>:   man

<u>Descriptive sentence</u>:   (2) I met a man who is kind to everyone.
<u>noun</u>:   man   <u>adjective clause</u>: who is kind to everyone

Put the **noun** first. Then follow it up with an **adjective clause**:
I met a <u>man who is kind to everyone.</u>
- It is a more descriptive sentence.
- A dependent clause, **who is kind to everyone**, has been created.

Sentence (3): I saw a big dog.   <u>adjective</u>: big   <u>noun</u>: dog

Descriptive sentence: I saw a dog that was big and ferocious.
<u>noun</u>: dog   <u>adjective clause</u>:   that was big and ferocious.

<u>Sentence (4)</u>: Tina threw a fun party.   <u>adjective</u>: fun   <u>noun</u>: party

Descriptive sentence: Tina threw a party that was amazingly fun and exciting.

noun: party   adjective clause: that was amazingly fun and exciting.

Practice Exercise: Change the adjective into an adjective clause.

1. Example: I saw a big elephant. **Noun**: elephant **adjective**: big
    Adjective clause: that was really big and majestic.

2. Sam watched a gorgeous sunset.   **Noun**: sunset **adjective**: gorgeous
    Adjective clause: _____.

3. Tina rode a big elephant.
    Adjective clause: _____.

4. I swam at a beautiful beach.
    Adjective clause: _____.

5. Phuket is a big island.
    Adjective clause: _____.

6. Wat Arun has many beautiful ornaments.
    Adjective clause: _____.

7. In Ko Kret, people can buy lovely pottery.
    Adjective clause: _____.

8. Prim bought Thai fruit at the bustling floating market.
    Adjective clause: _____.

9. We made our way down the river on a magnificent longboat.
    Adjective clause: _____.

10. The striped triggerfish swam by us.
    Adjective clause: _____.

11. Kanoon ate a spicy Tom Yam dish.
    Adjective clause: _____.

Short Story on Hindu Influence in Thailand

When trade routes from Thailand to India formed in the third century, Hindu ideas of religion, art, and royalty flowed into Thailand. Mon settlers also brought Hindu culture into Thailand, and when Thailand invaded the Khmer empire in 1431, they were impressed by the art and architecture of the Cambodians. The Khmers had magnificent temples based on the Hindu culture, so King Trailok reformed hai laws, architecture, and art, in line with Hindu notions. Even in present-day Thailand, many royal ceremonies and rituals are based on the Hindu rituals first adopted by ancient Thai kings.

<u>Definition</u>: **Ramayana** and **Ramakien** <u>à</u> based on or derived from **Rama**

The Hindu Influence in Thailand

Directions: Write new sentences by changing the adjectives into adjective clauses.

1. Hinduism was brought to Thailand by <u>Mon settlers</u>.

   _____.

2. Mons and Khmers were influenced by <u>Hindu merchants</u>.

   _____.

3. Thai kings based their laws on <u>Hindu law codes</u>.

   _____.

4. Brahman priests still conduct <u>Hindu rituals</u>.

   _____.

5. In 1431, King Trailok adopted artwork based on the <u>Hindu style</u>.

   _____.

6. Thai kings still base some ceremonies on <u>ancient, Hindu rituals</u>.

   _____.

7. Thai dance is still based on <u>Ramayana performances</u>.

   _____.

8. The Ramakien is the Thai version of the story of the <u>gods of Rama</u>.

   _____.

9. The Ramakien has been turned into a <u>dance</u> <u>drama</u>.

   _____.

10. There are 174 <u>Ramakien</u> <u>paintings and murals</u>.

    _____.

11. The Emerald Buddha Temple has many <u>Ramakien</u> <u>paintings</u>.

    _____.

12. The Ramakien has also been made into an <u>interesting</u> <u>puppet show</u>.

    _____.

13. The puppets are made from <u>stretched</u> <u>buffalo skins</u>.

    _____.

14. The puppets represent <u>different</u> <u>characters</u>.

    _____.

A2—Thai Forests and Jungles

"Wh" Questions—Making Questions with Auxiliary Verbs and Inversion

Auxiliary Verbs   - helping verbs
- used together with the main verb in a sentence
- add more meaning to a sentence

List of Auxiliary Verbs

be	can	could	dare	do	have	may
might	must	need	ought to	shall	should	
used to	will	would				

Five verbs in the list **can** be used as **full verbs.**
- These verbs are **be, do, dare, need,** and **have.**
- They **can** be **conjugated**. (**Be** can be conjugated to **is, am, are, was** or **were**, etc.)

Examples of sentences using **auxiliary verbs**:

(a)	Prim	**has been**	studying	for two hours.
(b)	Krit	**could have**	done	better on the test.
(c)	Peera	**should**	arrive	home before 10:00 p.m.

Questions can be made from these sentences with the following formula:

Original Sentence:

Subject + **(Auxiliary/Modal Verb)** + **(Auxiliary)** + **Main Verb**
Prim   **has**   **been**   **studying** for two hours.

Question:

(Auxiliary/Modal Verb) + **Subject** + **(Auxiliary)** + **Main Verb**
Has   Prim   **been**   **studying** for two hours?

Use the technique of **inversion** to make questions with auxiliary verbs.

Original Sentence:

Subject + **(Auxiliary/Modal Verb)** + **(Auxiliary)** + **Main Verb**
Krit   **could**   **have**   **done** better on the test.

Question:

(Auxiliary/Modal Verb) + **Subject** + **(Auxiliary)** + **Main Verb**
Could   Krit   **have**   **done** better on the test?

Practice Exercise: Use the technique of inversion to make questions out of the sentences.

1. Prang **will be going** to Phuket tomorrow.

   Will Prang **be going** to Phuket tomorrow?

2. Kanoon **must do** her homework tonight.

   _____.

3. Prim **should be arriving** soon.

   _____.

4. Tiger **will be absent** from school today.

   _____.

5. Toon **is used to studying** every night.

   _____.

6. Haddis **did play** soccer a lot before.

   _____.

7. Pao **has been practicing** her singing every day.

   _____.

Main Exercise—Thai Flowers, Fauna, and Animals in the Forests: Use the technique of inversion to make questions out of the sentences.

1. <u>Many crocodiles</u> **<u>are</u>** **<u>prowling</u>** the rivers close to the rain forests.

   <u>Are</u> <u>many crocodiles</u> **<u>prowling</u>** the rivers close to the rain forests?

2. <u>Creatures like the fiddler crab</u> **can climb** trees to catch their prey.

   _____.

3. <u>Mangrove trees in the forest</u> **have been able** to withstand the annual floods by using their own complex root systems.

   _____.

4. <u>Mangrove trees</u> **must trap** nutrients and soil with their roots for food.

   _____.

5. <u>Requirements to survive in the forest's ecosystem</u> **have produced** many different variations or types of organisms in a single species.

   _____.

6. <u>Anyone going into a forest</u> **must be** careful, because there are a lot of wild elephants and tigers walking in there.

   _____.

7. <u>Any animal</u> **can be eaten** by other animals in the forest.

   _____.

8. <u>Over two hundred tree species</u> **have been growing** in Thai forests for years.

   _____.

9. <u>Thailand</u> **does host** 10 percent of the world's fishes.

   _____.

10. <u>Mudskippers</u> **are able** to walk on the mud to chase prey.

    _____.

11. <u>Insects</u> **have been adapting** to the harsh jungle in order to survive.

    _____.

12. <u>Animals in the lower areas of the forests</u> **have survived** better than in the upper hills.

    _____.

13. <u>Plants in lower forests</u> **must be able** to regularly shed their leaves.

    _____.

14. <u>Over two hundred species of trees</u> **have** **been** **identified** in each acre of the Thai forest system.

    _____.

15. <u>Monkeys</u> **will** **call** out to each other to warn of incoming predators.

    _____.

16. <u>Wild animals</u> **will** **be** **able** to survive now, due to conservation efforts.

    _____.

17. <u>Jungles</u> **do** **become** very noisy when the sun comes up.

    _____.

18. <u>A lot of animals in the forest</u> **do** **have to** **come** out after dark, because they cannot bear the fierce heat of the jungle.

    _____.

A3—The Beaches of Ko Samui

Adjectives and Compound Words

Most compound words used in lessons I6 and I12 were nouns. In this lesson, all compound words are adjectives. The words in section A are hyphenated (-). The words in section B are not hyphenated (-).

First Objective: Match the adjectives in sections A and B with their definitions.

1. Quickly read the story (skim through the story on pages 164–165).

    Do this to try to understand the **gist**, or **main meaning**, of the story.

2. Return to sections A, B, and C. Figure out the meanings of the words.

3. You have to use your reasoning to figure out the meanings.

Example A: 5. shark infested   What is the meaning of this word?

Definition (a.) says: "refers to an ocean that has many, many **sharks**." So the answer for (5.) is (a.).

A.	1.	budget-priced	_____	a.	famous
	2.	emerald-green	_____	b.	a place with lots of trees, or a jungle, surrounding it
	3.	jungle-clad	_____	c.	a thing that costs little money
	4.	glistening-white	_____	d.	refers to a place or a thing that is so wonderful, that people are surprised how wonderful and beautiful it is
	5.	well-known	_a_	e.	refers to a body of water, or a forest, that has a beautiful green color to it
	6.	low-cost	_____	f.	a place or a thing that has many beautiful colours
	7.	kaleidoscope-filled	_____	g.	refers to sand on a beach that it is so white, that sunlight reflects off it
	8.	top-rated	_____	h.	the best, rated as the best
	9.	awe-inspiring	_____	i.	something that costs little money
B.	10.	olden flavou	_____	j.	refers to an ocean that has many, many sharks
	11.	bug infested	_____	k.	a place that is charming, due to its old traditional ways
	12.	shark infested	_____	l.	refers to a place with many, many bugs and mosquitoes

Ko Samui

1. Ko Samui is one of Thailand's **top-rated**, most **well-known** islands. It has many beaches, and it is not far from Bangkok. Visiting Ko Samui is therefore a very easy thing to do for people who live in Bangkok.

2. Chawaeng Beach is Ko Samui's most popular beach. It has **glistening-white** sand, which is enjoyed by many people throughout the year. A jagged rocky headland of rock separates Chawaeng Beach from Lamai Beach. Lamai is a beautiful beach, but it is harder to reach because of the big rock. One of the best things about these beaches is that their waters are not **shark-infested**.

3. There are other places on Ko Samui that are just as popular as Chawaeng Beach. Na Thon is the most well-known port on Ko Samui, so it is usually very busy. Lots of trees line the village of Na Muang, with its many **jungle-clad** hills. The jungle adds to the charm of Na Muang, which has an **olden-flavor** to it. The jungle and its animals are **awe-inspiring**, but the best things about the jungle is that it is not **bug-infested**. People can therefore feel comfortable in Na Muang, because they will not be bitten by mosquitoes.

4. The breathtaking waterfall of Na Muang is 105 feet high. The beautiful butterflies of Samui Butterfly Gardens also offer up a **kaleidoscope-filled** assortment of colors. The limestone caves at Mu Koh National Marine Park are surrounded by **emerald-green** water, so people love to visit Mu Koh not only for the caves but also for the pretty waters. These three places are some of the most heavily visited places by people who love nature.

5. The main reason people visit Ko Samui is for its lovely beaches. Bophut Beach is quite narrow, so there is not a lot of space for people to move around on it. The beaches next to Chawaeng have fewer people on them, but they are less developed, so there are fewer hotels and restaurants on them. The northern part of Chawsparsely-usedaeng Beach has lots of backpackers because there are many **budget-priced** hotels there. A visit to Ko Samui is therefore a fun, **low-cost** way to visit a beautiful island with many beautiful beaches.

Main Exercise: Answer the questions with one or two whole, proper sentences. The paragraph the topic appears in is in parentheses at the sentence's end.

1. What is a prominent feature of Chawaeng Beach on Ko Samui? (2)

   _____.

2. What separates Chawaeng Beach from Lamai Beach? (2)

   _____.

3. What is the name of the primary port on Ko Samui? (3)

    _____.

4. What lines the village of Na Muang? (3)

    _____.

5. What is on the hills of Na Muang? (3)

    _____.

6. How can you describe the waterfall at Na Huang? (4)

    _____.

7. What is 105 feet high? (4)

    _____.

8. Describe the beautiful butterflies of Samui Butterfly Gardens. (4)

    _____.

9. Why isn't there lots of space to move around on Bophut Beach? (5)

    _____.

10. Which islands have fewer people on them? (5)

    _____.

11. What surrounds the limestone caves at Mu Koh National Park? (4)

    _____.

A4—Monkeys, Elephants, and Dolphins

Declarative Sentences

It is essential to understand how grammar operates in a sentence. Grammatical units are the building blocks of sentences. A sentence is a unit that expresses an idea. Another definition of a sentence is expressed below.

Sentence: A **grammatical unit**, made up of either   (a) one **finite clause**, or
                                                                       (b) two or more **finite clauses**.

There are four types of sentences:

(1) **Declarative Sentences:** used when making statements
- The dog is brown.

(2) **Interrogative Sentences:** used when asking questions
- What color is the dog?

(3) **Imperative Sentence:** used when making orders, requests, or commands
- Tell Peter to bring the dog into the house.

(4) **Exclamatory Sentences:** used to make an exclamation
- That dog runs very fast!

Declarative sentences are the most common type of sentences.

A declarative sentence makes a statement.

Six basic clause patterns exist for declarative sentences. They are:

(1) **Subject + verb**

Elephants run.

Subject:	Elephants
Verb:	run

(2) **Subject + verb + object**

People ride elephants.
Subject: People
Verb: ride
Object: elephants

(3) **Subject + verb + indirect object + direct object**

People give elephants food.

(4) **Subject + verb + complement**

Elephants are animals.

(5) **Subject + verb + object + complement**

The elephant thrust him away.

(6) **Subject + verb + adverbial**

Elephants live in Thailand.

Complement: A word or a phrase used after a **verb** of **incomplete predication**. It is used to **complete a construction**.

Adverbial: Carries information about **when, where,** and **how** the **events** in a sentence **occur.**

Practice Exercise: Make four sentences with each of the first four clause patterns that exist for declarative sentences, using each picture.

These are the first four clause patterns for declarative sentences:

(1) Subject + verb
     Elephants run.

(2) Subject + verb + object
     People ride elephants.

(3) Subject + verb + indirect object + direct object
     People give elephants food.

(4) Subject + verb + complement
      Elephants are animals.

Sample Words: Subject: students, teachers, children, dogs, lions, elephants
                    Verb: teach, talk, learn, study, play, sleep, eat, roar, trumpet
                    Object: students, arithmetic, math, English
                    Direct Object: student
                    Complement: educated, responsible people, patient hard workers

Verb for Complement: are, is

(1) Subject +   verb
     Teachers   teach.
     Students   _____.
     Children   _____.
     I   _____.

(2) Subject +   verb +   object
     Teachers   teach   students.
     Teachers   teach   _____.
     Teachers   talk   to students.
     Teachers   talk   _____.
     Students   learn   _____.
     Students   _____   _____.

(3) Subject +   verb +   indirect object +   direct object
     Teachers   teach   students   English   .
     Teachers   teach   _____   _____.
     Teachers   talk   _____   _____.
     Teachers   talk   _____   _____.
     Students   learn   _____   _____.
     Students   _____   _____   _____.

(4) Subject +   verb +   complement
     Teachers   are   educated.
     Teachers   _____   _____.
     Teachers   _____   _____.
     Students   are   _____.
     Students   _____   _____.

Main Exercise: Make sentences from the following pictures.

A Monkey Climbing a Tree

(1)   Subject + verb
Monkeys run.

_____

_____

(2)   Subject + verb + object
Monkeys eat bananas.

_____

_____

(3)   Subject + verb + indirect object + direct object
People give monkeys bananas.

_____

_____

(4)   Subject + verb + complement
Monkeys are cute.

_____

_____

A Girl Riding an Elephant

(1)   Subject + verb

     Monkeys run.

     Monkeys play.

     _____

     _____

(2)   Subject + verb + object

     Monkeys eat bananas.

     _____

     _____

(3)   Subject + verb + indirect object + direct object

     People give monkeys bananas.

     _____

     _____

(4)   Subject + verb + complement

     Monkeys are cute.

     _____

     _____

An Elephant Eating Bananas

(1)   Subject + verb
      Monkeys run.
      Monkeys play.

      _____
      _____
      _____

(2)   Subject + verb + object
      Monkeys eat bananas.

      _____
      _____
      _____

(3)   Subject + verb + indirect object + direct object
      People give monkeys bananas.

      _____
      _____
      _____

(4)   Subject + verb + complement
      Monkeys are cute.

      _____
      _____
      _____

A Dolphin Jumping through a Hoop

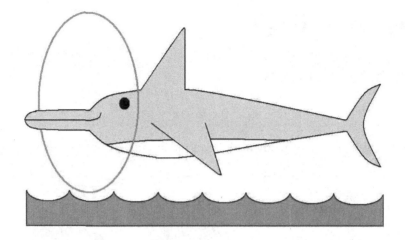

(1) Subject + verb

Dolphins jump.

_____

_____

(2) Subject + verb + object

Dolphins eat fish.

_____

_____

(3) Subject + verb + indirect object + direct object

People give monkeys bananas.

_____

_____

(4) Subject + verb + complement

Monkeys are cute.

_____

_____

A5—The Women of Thailand's Northern Tribes

Reading and Writing

This story tells the ways of life of women of Thailand's northern hill tribes.

Tribal Women called longnecks with neck brass rings

A Karen woman with her ornamental headdress

Children wear special caps.

The ornamental clothing of the women of Thailand's northern hill tribes.

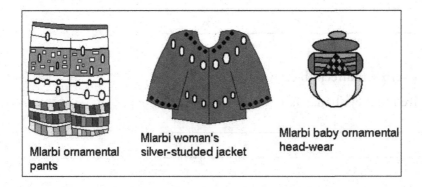

Mlarbi ornamental pants

Mlarbi woman's silver-studded jacket

Mlarbi baby ornamental head-wear

1. Below is a story about the ways of life and the rituals of the women of Northern Thailand hill tribes. **Skim** through the story first.

2. Then **read** and **understand** the meanings of the nouns, adjectives, verbs, and phrasal verbs.

3. Next, **read** the story in greater detail. Then **answer** the questions.

   This requires the **writing** of paragraphs.

4. Finally, **draw** one thing about the hill tribes.

Nouns

ancestor	– a person that proceeds another person or group
headdress	– an ornament that covers the head
jute	– the tough fiber or material from a certain Asian plant that is often used to make bags or ropes.
pelt	– the skin of an animal, especially with the fur removed, that is used to make coats and pants
rattan	– the stem of a long, tropical plant, used to make furniture
rite	– an important religious ceremony, done in a very definite way
ritual	– a method to perform a religious ceremony
tribe	– a class or group of people, especially if they are primitive or nomadic people, who share a common ancestry
amulet	– a type of ornament or stone that brings people good luck

Practice Exercise: Place the nouns correctly in the sentences.

ancestor	**headdress**	**jute**	**pelt**
rattan	**rite**	**ritual**	**tribe**

1. A group of people called the Mlarbi **tribe** build their houses out of bamboo.

2. Many of the jackets and pants that the women of hill tribes wear are made out of the _____ (s) of animals.

3. Much of the furniture made by tribes is made out of **rattan**.

4. Mlarbi women swing on trees. The ropes they use to swing on are made out of _____.

5. Every tribe wears a different _____ on their head.

6. The _____ (s) of the hill tribes started living on the hills hundreds of years ago.

7. The tribe's women wear special clothes in the religious ceremonies. This is a very special **rite** practiced by the women.

8. One of the women's _____ is to wear rings on their necks.

Adjectives

primitive	– simple, basic, uncomplicated, earliest, primary
fond	– to have affection for something, to love something

Directions: Practice using the adjectives by placing them in the correct sentences.

1. The ways of life of the hill tribes are very _____.

2. The Mlarbi women are _____ of wearing special clothing.

Adjectives + Nouns

edible roots	– underground part of plants that can be eaten
evil spirit	– a supernatural being, like a ghost, demon, or fairy, that has an evil soul
embroidered costumes	– costumes with special patterns sewn into them
fringed headdress	– headdress that has ornaments, cords, or threads hanging or emblazoned on it
monsoon season	– the rainy season
medicinal plant roots	– the underground part of plants used for medicines
nipah palm leaves	– a palm leaf that can be eaten
silver stud	– a small piece of silver used to decorate clothing
silver-studded jackets	– a jacket with silver studs placed in them

Directions: Place the **adjectives + nouns** in the correct sentences.

edible roots	**embroidered costume**	**evil spirit**
fringed headdress	**medicinal plant roots**	**monsoon season**
nipah palm leaves	**silver studs**	**silver-studded jackets**

1. Women decorate their hats and jackets with **silver studs**.

2. Mlarbi women often wear a _____ on their head.

3. Tribes perform ceremonies to keep _____(s) away.

4. The rainy season is called the _____.

5. Tribal people can eat _____, or they can use them to make medicine.

6. Tribal women wear _____. These jackets also have other patterns sewn into them.

7. An **embroidered costume** is a costume with special decorations on it.

8. _____ are used to make household goods. Their leaves can be used for so many things.

9. Thai hill tribes don't buy medicine at the drugstore. Instead, they use _____ to make their medicines.

Verbs

lurk	– to lie hidden
gather	– accumulate, bring together into one place
surround	– to encircle something, to extend completely around it, on all sides
stretch	– to draw or extend something, so as to make it longer
perform	– to carry out an action, to do, to execute
swinging	– to go back and forth on something
build	– to erect, to make, to construct
vibrate	– to shake, to move back and forth in a rapid and repetitive way

Directions: Practice using the verbs by placing them in the correct sentences

build	**gather**	**lurk**	**perform**
stretch	**surround**	**swing**	**vibrate**

1. Evil spirits often **lurk** in the jungle.

2. Mlarbis _____ their houses out of bamboo.

3. The jungles _____ the houses of the tribes.

4. The tribes can hear the ground _____ when enemies are coming to attack. To do this, tribe people put their ears on the ground.

5. The tribes ____**gather**_____ their food and supplies in the jungle.

6. The brass rings that women wear on their necks _____ the necks and make them very long.

7. Mlarbi women _____ off trees for three days at New Year's.

8. Tribes have very specific rituals, or <u>rites</u>, that they _____.

Phrasal Verbs

keep these evil spirits away	– prevent the evil spirit from coming to you
adhere to	– believe in, stick with
pressed close	– to exert pressure onto something, so that it comes very close to you

Practice using the **phrasal verbs** by placing them in the correct sentences

adhere to   **keep away**   **pressed close**

1. The tribes keep their ears _____ to the ground, so they can hear enemies who are coming to attack them.

2. Thai tribes have very special rites they _____.

3. Tribal women perform special rituals to _____ evil spirits _____.

The Women of Northern Thailand's Hill Tribes

A number of primitive tribes live in the hills of Northern Thailand. Tribal people build their homes from the bamboo they **gather** in the jungles, and they also **gather** their medicine and food in the jungles that **surround** the villages. The tribes therefore have to make sure that evil spirits that live in the jungles will not harm them when they go into the jungle.

Tribal people believe evil spirits **lurk** outside their villages, so they do things to **keep** the evil spirits **away**. These things are called rituals. The women in Thailand's tribes have very specific rituals, or rites, that they either perform or **adhere to**. The women of the Padaung tribe from the Mae Hong Song area wear brass rings around their necks. These rings **stretch** the women's necks and make them very long. The women of the Ahha tribe, in the Chiang Rai area, celebrate New Year's by **swinging** on ropes for three days during the monsoon season to make sure that crops grow well. Women in all tribes wear special clothes and costumes, like silver-studded jackets or fringed headdresses, when they celebrate or perform their rituals. During these rites, the women pray to their ancestors to help protect them against evil spirits.

Women in all tribes also make their own clothes. They are all especially **fond** of beads. The women of the Meo tribe wear special headwear, and so do the women of the Acha tribe. Women of the Meo, Acha, and Yao tribes make specialized embroidered costumes, amulets, jackets, bags, and headdresses. The women are **fond** of using silver, seeds, coins, monkey fur, and chicken feathers in their creations. The women of all hill tribes also have traditional clothing they wear all the time, when they are not performing their ceremonies.

The Mlabri tribe, also known as "People of the Forest," **build** their homes from banana leaves. When the leaves turn yellow and **dry out**, the Mlabri move and then build new homes out of new banana leaves. Thais call the Mlabri the "Phi Toy Luoy," or "Spirits of the Yellow Leaves," because they build their houses out of banana leaves. The tribes wait for the leaves to dry out before they build their houses out of them. The Mlabri women **gather** edible roots, fruits, ferns, and medicinal plant roots to eat or for use as medicines. The women also gather rattan, nipah palm leaves, and jute for making household goods and furniture. The men hunt animals, which provides food and materials to make pelts. The men also fish, trap crabs, and climb trees to get bird eggs.

The Mlabri sleep with their ears on the ground, and this is for a very good reason. When their ears are **pressed close** to the earth, the Mlabri can hear approaching enemies or dangerous animals. The ground will **vibrate** when an animal or an enemy approaches, so these noises wake the people up and allow them to run away to safety in the face of danger. The Mlabri must therefore always keep moving to stay alive.

Directions: Answer the questions based on the paragraphs above. Do not just copy from the story.

1. What do the Mlarbi women do with bamboo leaves?

   Sample Answer:

   The Mlarbi are sometimes called the "People of the Forest." The Mlarbi women gather vegetables and fruits from the forest, but they also gather different types of **leaves** and fruits from the forest to make household goods. One special thing the women gather is **banana leaves**. The women use the banana leaves to build new homes. They wait until the banana leaves turn yellow and dry out before using them. Thai people sometimes call the Mlarbi the "Spirits of the Yellow Leaves" because the Mlarbi use banana leaves to build their Homes.

2. Do the Mlarbi own TVs or computers?

3. Name some things that Thailand's tribes do to protect themselves from evil spirits.

4. How do the women of the Ahha tribe celebrate New Year's?

5. Do northern Thai tribes buy their clothes at shopping malls?

6. What do women in various Thai tribes do to decorate their clothing and their household goods?

7. What do you think of the brass neck rings the Padaung women wear?

8. What special name is given to the Mlarbi people? Why?

Draw one of the following things:

1. A woman and a baby of one of the tribes of Northern Thailand

2. A Mlarbi house that is made from banana leaves

3. A woman dressed in her special clothes and headdress

4. The brass neck rings worn by the Mlarbi women

5. Anything you want to draw, but it must be about the women from one of the tribes

A6—Sukhothai and Ayuttyaha

Hyphenated Compound Words
Thailand's Ancient Capitals

Before doing this exercise   (a)   review the following words:
                             (b)   refer to appendix C, an introduction to compound words.

Nouns

rampart   – the piece of land that surrounds an embankment
embankment   – something, like a piece of land, that is raised higher, so as to prevent water
                   from coming in
moat   – a deep and wide water-filled trench that surrounds a castle
irrigation   – the act of supplying water to an area that lacks water
merchant   – a person who buys or sells items for a profit
opulence   – extreme wealth, affluence, luxury
ruins   – the things that remain after something is destroyed
charm   – an alluring or fascinating feature of something

Adjectives

intricate   – complicated, difficult to understand or to follow
idyllic   – refers to a time in the past when things were simple and pleasant

Directions: Place the nouns and adjectives with the correct sentences.

<u>Nouns:</u>   irrigation   merchant   **opulence**   rampart   ruins

<u>Adjectives:</u>   **intricate**   idyllic

1. The _____ that surrounded the castle provided protection against enemy attack.

2. The _____ sold his things in the busiest part of town.

3. The farmer's land would have been dry without _____.

4. The **intricate** system around the farmer's field protected it from flooding.

158

5. The **opulence** of the furniture, paintings, and decorations inside the castle suggested that the royal family was very wealthy.

6. The _____ in the ancient city of Ayuttyaha refer back to a more **(adjective)** _____ era in Thai history.

Verbs

abandon   – to desert, to leave, to give over
converge   – to meet, to come together, to move toward one point
found   – to discover, to set up, to establish
launch   – to start something
proclaim   – to announce in an official way
restore   – to rebuild after being ruined
wane   – to diminish in size or importance

Directions: Place the verbs with the correct sentences.

Verbs: **abandon**   **converge**   **found**   **proclaim**
            restored **wane**

1. Sukhothai was _____ **ed** in 1238.

2. Many Thai kings _____ **ed** new laws in their speeches.

3. When Sukhothai **waned** in importance, the city was **abandoned** and Thailand's capital was moved to Ayuttyaha.

4. Three rivers _____, or meet, at Bangkok.

5. Many temples in Ayuttyaha were _____ and made new again after Burma attacked Ayuttyaha in 1757.

Compound Words

Compound words consist of two different words joined together to make a new word. The compound words in this section have a hyphen (-) between them. Match the compound words with their definitions.

1. man-made   _____   A.   respected, reputable, famous
2. ruined-nature   _____   B.   massive; very, very big
3. super-huge   _____   C.   prosperous, doing very well
4. temple-building   _____   D.   made by humans

5. pre-eminent _____   E. something that has been destroyed and is left in ruins
6. well-thought-of _____   F. erecting or building temples
7. well-to-do _____   G. old ways, ancient, not modern
8. old-fashioned _____   H. supreme, ultimate, unmatched

<u>Note</u>: **<u>pre-eminent</u>**: **pre** ends with an **e**, and **eminent** begins with an **e**. Hyphens are used in these cases to separate the **two e vowels**.

Compound words in the story that do not have a hyphen (-):

1. township _____   A. a drop, a fall, a decline
2. ransacked _____   B. the main part of a town
3. downturn __A__   C. located up the river from some
4. golden age _____   D. something that is remaining from a previous time
5. downstream _____   E. located down the river from some place
6. leftover _____   F. a prosperous time or era
7. upstream _____   G. destroyed thoroughly

Sukhothai and Ayuttyaha, Two Ancient Thai Capitals

Many compound words were introduced above. The definitions of these compound words are placed in the story below. Place the appropriate compound word next to the bold definitions.

downstream	**downturn**	**golden age**
leftover	**man-made**	**old-fashioned**
pre-eminent	**ransacked**	**ruined-nature**
super-huge	**temple-building**	**township**
upstream	**well-thought-of**	**well-to-do**

Sukhothai and Ayuttyaha are two ancient Thai capitals. Sukhothai, the oldest of the two capitals, is 460 kilometers (275 miles) north of Bangkok. The city was founded in 1238, when King Intharathit proclaimed Thailand's independence from the Khmer empire. The Khmer empire covered most of Southeast Asia before 1238, but its power began waning in the twelfth century. By the thirteenth century, Khmer power weakened, so many lands it possessed declared independence. The previous Khmer empire is now known as Cambodia.

Sukhothai is supplied by a number of rivers, so its former king, King Ramhkamheawell, once proclaimed his city had lots of fish in its waters and lots of rice in its fields. Sukhothai has many ancient temples, but by 1438, Ayuttyaha had become the (**most powerful**) _____ city in Thailand. The (**prosperous time**) _____ of (**building new temples**) _____ in Sukhothai lasted for only two hundred years, because in 1438, Ayuttyaha became Thailand's new capital. The most (**famous**) _____ king of Sukhothai was King Ramhkamheang. The king made some changes in the Thai language, and also promoted Theravada Buddhism throughout the kingdom.

Old Sukhothai is surrounded by ancient walls, and the inner **(town)** _____ is protected by rows of eastern ramparts and two moats. Sukhothai was ruled by the Khmer empire prior until 1238, so there are still a few **(remaining)** _____ Hindu temples in the city. When the Thais started building their own Buddhist temples in Sukhothai, the Khmers abandoned the city. After the Khmers left, the intricate canals and irrigation systems in the city were neglected by the Thais, so Sukhothai experienced a **(decline)** _____.

Ayuttyaha became Thailand's capital in 1350 and remained the capital until 1767. The Burmese often launched attacks on Ayuttyaha and were finally successful in 1767, when they **(destroyed)** _____ the city. Before this attack, Ayuttyaha had grown in importance and had become a **(very, very big)** _____ city. By the eighteenth century, Ayuttyaha had a population of over one million people. At that time, it was bigger than London.

Ayuttyaha is only eighty-five kilometers (fifty-five miles) **(up the river from)** _____ from Bangkok, and it is built where three rivers converge. A canal was dug around the city many centuries ago, so the city is classified as an island. Many palaces and temples were built along Ayuttyaha's **(made by humans)** _____ canals, and many of these palaces and temples still stand today. Due to the presence of the canals, it is sometimes called the "Venice of the East." A river connects Bangkok and Ayuttyaha, so boat trips can be made from Bangkok on a modern boat or traditional barge.

Prince U Thong founded Ayuttyaha in 1350. The prince later took the name King Ramathibod I. By 1600, Ayuttyaha was the richest city in Asia, so its citizens were very **(prosperous)** _____. Merchants would come from all parts of Asia, the Middle East, and Europe to trade in Ayuttyaha. Europeans wrote many stories about the wealth and opulence of Ayuttyaha. Thirty-three different kings ruled Ayuttyaha between 1350 and 1757. The Burmese launched many attacks on the city, and the city was finally destroyed in 1757. After the 1757 attacks, most of Ayuttyaha lay in ruins.

After 1757, the Thai royal family moved the capital **(down the river from)** _____ to Bangkok, at the mouth of the Chao Praya River. Ayuttyaha still remains an important historical city, and it is now known as Ayuttyaha Historical Park. Some temples have been restored or rebuilt, but the **(destroyed look)** _____ of many temples adds to the city's charm. Ayuttyaha is easy to get to by boat, train, or bus from Bangkok, but the most fun way to go is by taking an inexpensive train from Bangkok. Using this **(old way)** _____ form of travel brings back the idyllic days of train travel.

A7—The 2005 Indian Ocean Earthquake

Phrasal Verbs

In this lesson, twelve phrasal verbs are introduced. Do the exercises in appendix A before attempting this lesson. Then match the nouns, adjectives, and noun phrases with their definitions. Refer to a dictionary or the Internet for assistance.

Directions: Match the nouns with their definitions.

1.	corpses	____	a.	uninjured, unharmed, to escape harm
2.	wildlife	____	b.	dead bodies
3.	unscathed	_a_	c.	animals who are not household pets

Directions: Match the **adjectives + nouns** with their definitions

1.	human casualties	_c_	a.	sounds that warn of impending danger
2.	sensory abilities	____	b.	the ability to sense through our senses
3.	underwater rupture	____	c.	a number of people who have died
4.	sound waves	____	d.	sound
5.	infrasound or	____	e.	sound at infrasonic wavelengths infrasonic sound
6.	low tones	____	f.	sound made of low-frequency waves
7.	early-warning sound	____	g.	sensors in animals' or people's joints that warn of possible danger
8.	ground vibration	____	h.	the shaking of the ground
9.	red flags	_J_	i.	a rupture or crack on the ocean floor
10.	Pacinian corpuscles	____	j.	something that warns of danger

Directions: Match the **phrasal verbs** with their definitions.

1.	bringing about	_b_	a.	become excited
2.	get crazy	____	b.	causing
3.	going on	____	c.	turns out to be okay
4.	move up	____	d.	gave them a warning
5.	pick up	____	e.	happening
6.	pin down	____	f.	to ignore something

7.	run for	_g_	g.	move to a higher elevation
8.	scatter away	___	h.	to sense, to notice
9.	screen it out	___	i.	run away to another place
10.	spread out	_k_	j.	to understand, know the answer to
11.	tipped them off	___	k.	spread out in all directions
12.	works out	___	l.	to run away quickly from a place

The Indian Ocean Tsunami of December 26, 2004

Directions: Place the nouns and phrasal verbs in the proper spaces in the paragraphs.

corpses   **unscathed**   **wildlife**

(1) Reports from Thailand after the tsunami of December 26, 2004 say that most animals seem to have survived **unscathed** despite the enormous number of _____, (16,000 deaths) and rising. Phuket Island has buffalo, elephants, and monkeys, but no animal _____ were found. Only thirty of 250 tourist vehicles on the beach were found. Did animals sense the oncoming tsunami and then flee to safety?

get crazy   **pin down**   **tipped them off**   **pick up**

(2) There's a good chance the wildlife knew trouble was coming. Animals can act strangely before natural disasters occur, but scientists find it hard to _____ how they do this. Sometimes animals _____ before an earthquake; sometimes they don't. Here's what we know: animals have sensory abilities different from our own, and they might have _____ **them** _____ to the shaking. It's possible they heard the quake before the tsunami came. The underwater rupture likely made sound waves known as infrasound or infrasonic sound. These low tones can be created by meteors, volcanic eruptions, avalanches, or earthquakes. Humans can't _____, infrasound, but many animals can.

bringing about   **spread out**

(3) A second early-warning sign the animals might have felt is ground vibration. In addition to _____ the tsunamis, the earthquake created huge vibrational waves that _____ from the epicenter on the ocean and traveled through the earth. Known as Rayleigh waves (Lord Rayleigh predicted their existence in 1885), these vibrations move through the ground like waves move on the surface of the ocean. They travel ten times faster than the speed of sound. The waves would have reached Thailand hours before the water of the tsunami.

move up   **ran for**   **scatter away**

(4) Mammals, birds, and insects can feel Rayleigh waves move through their bodies, but some animals, like snakes, put their ears to the ground to feel them. Phuket's animals might have felt the Rayleigh waves and _____ higher ground. Animals sometimes _____ from a place where they are disturbed. So, in this case, "away" may have meant away from the sea. Or maybe it's not so accidental. It's easy to imagine that if the ground beneath your feet starts moving, then you will run away as fast as you can, or _____ to higher ground.

going on   **screen it out**   **works out**

(5) What about humans? What are our red flags? People do feel infrasound, but we don't necessarily know that that's what we're feeling. Some people feel afraid or even feel religious feelings. We also experience Rayleigh waves in special sensors in our joints (called Pacinian corpuscles) that can feel infrasound. Sadly, it seems we don't pay attention to the information we get. Maybe we _____ **it** _____ because there's so much _____ before our eyes and in our ears. Humans often have a lot of things on their minds, and usually that _____ okay.

Exercise: Answer the following questions in one or two sentences.

1. What is a red flag? Describe the latest red flag you sensed.

2. Use the three phrasal verbs below to make three sentences:

    screen out   **tip off**   **pin down**

3. Is it a good thing to tame wildlife, or should we just let animals roam around in the wild or in the jungle?

4. If the humans on Phuket saw the animals running away just before the tsunami hit, why didn't the humans run away too?

5. How did the snakes sense the sound waves from the tsunami?

6. How fast did the sound waves travel through the ground after the earthquake?

7. Draw a picture of the animals on Phuket. Show how they heard the sound waves from the tsunami and then how they ran or flew away later. Label your drawing.

A8—Thai Cities, Towns, and Islands

Adjective Clauses

Adjective clauses can be used to:

(1) give information about nouns

(2) identify or describe indefinite pronouns such as someone, somebody, something, another, or others.

In most cases, the adjective clause directly follows the noun or pronoun it is identifying or describing.

Sentences with adjective clauses are seen as a combination of two sentences.

Example: I watched a movie. It was about a dragon.

Now change these two sentences so they   – are one sentence
                                            – have an adjective clause

I watched a movie that was about a dragon.

Independent Clause: I watched a movie
Adjective Clause: that was about a dragon

Note: Independent clauses are complete sentences, while dependent clauses are not complete sentences. A dependent clause must be attached to an independent clause.

In the following exercise, two complete sentences, or independent clauses, are grouped together. Students will change one of the sentences into an independent clause and then combine the two sentences to make one sentence. Students will use the words **who**, **which**, **whose,** or **that** to connect the sentences.

Rules: Use: **who, whose,** or **that** to refer to people.
            Use: **which, whose,** or **that** to refer to places or things.

That is less formal than **who** and **which**.

Example:

I have a friend. She loves to shop.
I have a friend **who** loves to shop.

165

Tina has a dog. The dog's name is Rex.
Tina has a dog **whose** name is Rex.

Practice Exercise: Combine the two sentences into one sentence by changing the second sentence into an adjective clause. Use **that**, **whose**, **who,** or **which** to connect the sentences.

1. I swam in an ocean. The water was warm.

   I swam in an ocean **whose** water was warm.

2. I rode an elephant. It swayed back and forth as it walked.

3. The dugong is a strange-looking animal. It lives in the ocean.

4. The dolphin is a mammal. It swims very fast.

5. The crocodile has sharp teeth. Its bite is dangerous.

Main Exercise: Combine two sentences to make one sentence by changing the second sentence into an adjective clause. Use the words **that, who, whose, where,** or **which** to connect the sentences.

1. Bangkok is a big city. It has a lot of shopping malls.

2. Chang Mai is a charming city. It attracts a lot of tourists.

3. Ayuttyaha is an ancient city. It has a lot of ancient temples.

4. Ko Phangan has a beach. It is famous for its full-moon party.

5. Ko Phangan also has some coral reefs. They are full of beautiful fish.

6. Ko Phi Phi Don and Ko Phi Phi Ley are twin islands. They both have beautiful beaches.

    _____

7. Hat Khlong Khong is a beach. It is famous for its snorkeling.

    _____

8. Many tribes live in Northern Thailand. They live mostly in the mountains.

    _____

9. Doi Inthanon is a mountain. It is Thailand's highest mountain.

    _____

10. James Bond Island is a famous island. James Bond filmed a movie there.

    _____

11. Market Chatguchak is a market. It is the world's biggest flea market.

    _____

12. Samut Prakan has a crocodile farm. It is home to fish and crocodiles.

    _____

13. The crocodile farm has a shop. It sells crocodile skin handbags and shoes.

    _____

14. The crocodile handlers wrestle crocodiles. The crocodiles are dangerous.

    _____

15. Ko Chang is a beautiful island. It is Thailand's second largest island.

    _____

16. Khlong Chao is a waterfall. It attracts many visitors.

    _____

17. Khao Wang is a huge palace. It was the summer residence of King Mongkut.

    _____

A9—Animism and Rituals in Thai Life

Phrasal Verbs

Match the following nouns or noun phrases with their definitions:

Part A

1. animism   <u>c</u>   a. a form of Hinduism from one of the four Hindu castes, also known as the sacerdotal caste

2. amulets   ____   b. a charm, often worn around the neck, to protect a person from evil spirits

3. Brahmanism   ____   c. the belief in the existence of spirits

4. belief system   ____   d. a formal act or ritual, performed in a predetermined way or manner

5. ceremony   ____   e. a set of tenets, doctrines, or creeds that a specific group believes in

Part B

6. offering   ____   f. a type of power that is believed to be miraculous and that exists beyond anything that is natural

7. tribal people   ____   g. something that is offered, such as a gift, for a spirit

8. ritual   <u>h</u>   h. a certain method that is used when performing a ceremony

9. shrine   ____   i. a sacred place where shamans or healers perform ceremonies

10. supernatural   ____   j. a clan or group of people from rural powers or primitive places that have common ancestry or customs

Do the exercises in appendix A before doing this lesson.

Directions: Place the following definitions next to the appropriate phrasal verbs.

1. come from _____   a. all the hair is shaven off

2. bring about ___<u>c</u>___   b. bring them

3.   presented with _____   c.   cause

4.   carried out _____   d.   composed of

5.   dug up _____   e.   cut hair right down to the skin

6.   packed full of ____i_____   f.   done

7.   takes place _____   g.   erect or build

8.   take in _____   h.   excavated

9.   strewn throughout _____   i.   filled with

10. put up _____   j.   given

11. carried out _____   k.   done

12. shaved clean _____   l.   occurs

13. attend to _____   m.   originate

14. shaved off _____   n.   to place upon something

15. put on _____   o.   spread around

16. bless them with _____   p.   take care of an important matter

17. made up of _____   q.   watch, to observe

Animism in Thai Life

Directions: Choose the most appropriate phrasal verbs in the parentheses. Refer to the phrasal verbs listed above for assistance.

Most Thais are Buddhists who believe in life after death. More important for Thai people, though, is their belief in spirits. Some spirits are good, and some are bad, and a spirit may **(come from / put on)** <u>come from</u> a dead person, or a mountain, tree, or river. Thais also believe that if spirits are ignored, then this can **(presented with / bring about)** _____bad luck for a person. Spirits must therefore be made happy so that spirits can make a person's life better instead of making it worse.

   Thais perform a number of ceremonies or rituals to appease spirits in the spirit world. In the ceremonies, the spirits are **(put on / presented with)** _____ things like flowers, candles, food, incense, or carved elephants. Dances and performances are also **(packed full of / carried out)** _____, to please the spirits. A common thing done when a building or a house is being built is to build a miniature spirit house next to the new house or new building. Thais believe that spirits in the ground are disturbed when the ground is **(dug up / carried out)** _____, so the miniature spirit house must be built for spirits to live in during this time. The miniature house is also **(packed full of / put up)** _____ things like offerings or gifts, in order to make the spirits happy.

The rice spirit is the most powerful spirit. A special ceremony **(takes place / carried out)** _____ in May to honor the rice spirit on the royal palace grounds in Bangkok. This is done to bless the rice spirit, to make sure the rice crop is plentiful after rice seeds are planted. The king **(carries out / takes in)** _____ the rice ceremony, where a pair of sacred oxen plow a field with a sacred plow. Rice seeds are then **(dug up / strewn throughout)** _____ this field as part of the ceremony. Tribal people in Thailand's villages also have their own rice ceremonies. The ceremony is led by a village spiritual leader. Villagers also **(put up / made up of)** _____ a shrine in the rice fields, and gifts are left for the rice spirit in the shrine.

Witch doctors, monks, and spirit doctors often perform the special ceremonies that are **(bless them with / carried out)** _____ to appease spirits. This is important, because if any part of the ceremony is done incorrectly, then Thais believe the spirit will not answer their prayers. It is assumed that only witch doctors, monks, and spirit doctors can correctly perform a ceremony. When a child is born, for example, a special rite must be performed in order to protect a child's soul from evil spirits. If a witch doctor, monk, or spirit doctor does not perform this special ceremony, then it is believed that the baby might be cursed for the rest of his or her life.

One of the most important rites for a boy **(attend to / takes place)** _____ in the tonsure ceremony. The boy's head is **(shaved clean / put on)** _____, except for a thick lock of hair on top of the boy's head. The boy's parents **(come from / attend to)** _____ bringing their son to a Brahman temple, to have the top part of his hair **(shaved off / dug up)** _____. A mark is then **(made up of / put on)** _____ the boy's forehead by a Brahman priest.

Amulets are an important part of a Thai's belief system. Amulets protect Thais from evil spirits, and Thais believe that amulets **(bless them with / attend to)** _____ good luck. The most popular amulets are of Buddha, or portraits of famous kings or monks. Others amulets are **(dug up / made up of)** _____ tiger teeth or animal parts. Amulets are thought to bring good luck and to have supernatural powers, so warriors wear them in battle, and businessmen wear them when they negotiate business deals. Thais do all these things to protect themselves from evil spirits.

A10—Hotel Phuket

Conversation

The main aim of this lesson is to practice speaking.

Part 1: Students will form pairs and practice the conversation activities.

Part 2: Students will make reservations for hotels and their activities.

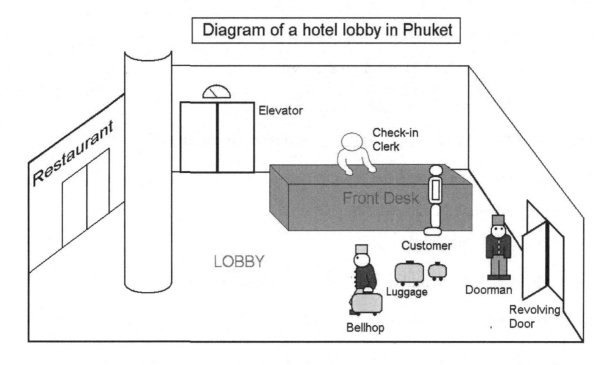
Diagram of a hotel lobby in Phuket

Part 1

C – Customer	DM – Doorman	BH – Bellhop
CC – Check-in Clerk	Lobby	Luggage

Directions: In conversations 1, 2, and 3, students will form pairs and then practice speaking to each other. In conversation 1, for example, one student will be the customer, and the other student will be the doorman. The students will then switch roles.

Conversation 1

C: Where is the front desk?v

DM: Inside the hotel, in the lobby. Just walk through the revolving door.

C: Thank you.

BH: Hi, welcome to the hotel. Let me take your luggage.

C: Where is the front desk?

BH: In the back of the lobby.

C: Thank you.

CC: Welcome to the hotel. Do you have a reservation?

C: Yes, I do. My name is _____.

CC: Okay, (Mr. / Mrs.) _____, your room number is 1005.

C: What kind of room do I have?

CC: You have reserved a suite. Here are your keys.

C: Thank you. Where is the elevator?

CC: It's to your left. The bellhop will carry your luggage for you.

C: Thank you.

Conversation 2   A – person 1   B – person 2

A: Where are you going?

B: I'm going to the pool to swim. Would you like to come?

A: Sure, but I would also like to go the gym. Let's go to the gym first, and then we can swim.

B: Good idea. What are you going to wear? I'm am going to wear my shorts and tank top.

A: I'm going to wear my purple sweatshirt and purple sweatpants.

B: Great. Its 3:00 p.m. now. Let's come back in two hours. We can shower and then have dinner. What are you going to wear to dinner?

A: I think I will just wear shorts and a simple shirt.

B: I'm going to do the same as you. I have some comfortable walking shorts.

A: Sounds great. What do you want to have for dinner?

B: I would like to have steak and potatoes. How about you?

A: I will be very hungry. Why don't we have the buffet instead?

B: Sure. Let's go to the gym now. Then we can go eat at the buffet.

A: Sounds great. Let's go!

Conversation 3—Room Service   A – room service   B – customer

A: Hello. Room service. May I help you please?

B: Yes, I'd like to order some food.

A: What would you like to have?

B: I'd like to order   beef, pork, steak, lamb chops, fish, barbequed ribs, chicken, pizza, pasta, pad Thai, Thom Yam
(Choose two items, one for each person.)
potatoes **or** rice **or** Vegetables two salads

A: What would you like to drink?

B: Two cokes. **(Or beer, wine, champagne, coffee, tea.)**

A: Let me see, that's   _____

_____

_____

and _____.

That will be $ _____.

What is your room number?

B: Its 1005. How long will that be?

A: It will take about thirty minutes.

B: Okay, thanks.

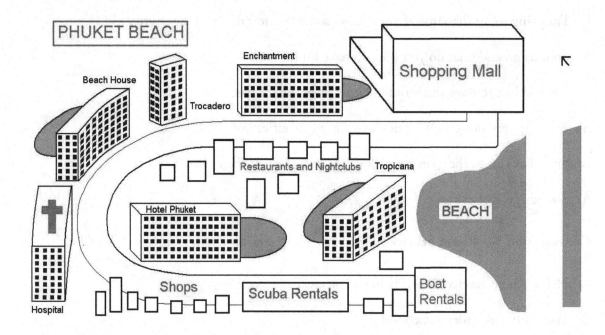

Part 2

The picture on the previous page is a representation of Phuket's beach with hotels, restaurants, shops, a shopping mall, several services, and a beach.

Students will: 1.   Review the services each hotel offers.
2.   Then students will pair up and ask each other questions about the hotels and their services.

The types of questions students will ask each other are on pages 198–199. These questions will involve using the words **is, are, does, do, when how, who, where, which, how.**

Sample questions and answers might be:

<u>Question, Student 1</u>:   **Does** Hotel Trocadero have a swimming pool?
<u>Answer, Student 2</u>:   **No**, Hotel Trocadero **does not** have a swimming pool.

<u>Question, Student 1</u>:   **Is** Hotel Enchantment next to the shopping mall?
<u>Answer, Student 2</u>:   **Yes**, it is right next to the shopping mall.

Each student can refer to table 1, which gives information about each hotel and the services they offer. Services that a hotel can offer include gyms, restaurants, twenty-four-hour room service, and airport shuttles.

At the bottom of table 1 is the price per week to stay at each of the hotels.

Tropicana	Enchantment	Trocadero	Beach House	Hotel Phuket
$2,400	$2,000	$1,600	$1,200	$1,000

Hotel Tropicana is the most expensive, and Hotel Phuket is the least expensive. Students can choose their hotel depending on how much money they want to have leftover to do other things. If a student, for example, wants to Jet Ski a lot or do a lot of shopping, then he or she will choose a lower priced hotel like Beach House or Hotel Phuket. If a student would like more services and to enjoy free meals at the hotel, then he or she might choose Tropicana. The conversations can become interesting in this way, because students can ask all types of questions about the hotels.

Each student will take turns answering or asking the questions, at one time being the **reservation agent (RA)**, and at another time being the **customer (CU)**. The following can be a typical conversation between an **RA** and a **CU**:

RA: Hello, may I help you?

CU: Yes, I would like to ask about the hotels in Phuket.

RA: Okay, we have five hotels. They range in price from $2,400 to $1,000 per week.

CU: Yes, I'd like a budget-priced hotel because we want to do a lot of shopping and windsurfing.

RA: Okay, that sounds great. There are two hotels, the Beach House at $1,200 per week, and Hotel Phuket at $1,000 per week.

(Now the student can look at table 1 to start asking questions about the services. Sample questions and answers are placed below table 1.)

CU: **Is** there a scuba-diving area close to these hotels?

(The reservation agent can look at the map of Phuket and the sample answer given to answer this question).

Sample question and answer given below:

Is there a scuba-diving area close to the hotel?

1.   Yes, there is a scuba-diving area on the northeast side of the beach.
2.   No, you must walk ten minutes to get to the scuba area.

RA: No, you must walk ten minutes to get to the scuba area, but Hotel Phuket is a bit closer to the scuba area on the beach.

CU: **Does** either hotel have a pool?

RA: Yes, Hotel Phuket has a pool, but Beach House doesn't have one.

CU: **Does** either hotel have a shuttle to the mall?

RA: Beach House has a shuttle to the mall, but Hotel Phuket does not.

CU: **Does** either hotel have childcare?

RA: No, neither of the hotels has childcare.

CU: **Do** either of the hotels serve free meals?

RA: Yes, both hotels have free breakfast and lunch, but the price for dinner is not included.

This is one of the sample questions in the "**is**" section:

Is there a gym or an exercise area in the hotel?
1.   Yes, there is a gym at the hotel.
2.   No, there is no gym at your hotel, but you can go to some of the other hotels and pay to use their gyms.

CU: **Is** there a gym or an exercise area in the hotel?

RA: No, there is no gym at your hotel, but you can go to some of the other hotels and pay to use their gym.

This is one of the sample questions in the "**are**" section:

Are scuba rentals or boat rentals available at the hotel?
1.   Yes, scuba rentals are available at the hotel.
2.   No, but there are many places to rent scuba gear, and the rentals cost less at these places than at the other hotels.

CU: Are scuba rentals or boat rentals available at the hotel?

RA: No, but there are many places to rent scuba gear, and the rentals cost less at these places than at the other hotels.

CU: Are tours included in the price?

RA: Yes, you can take one free tour to Krabi, and there are unlimited rides to Kata Beach.

CU: When are the meals served?

RA: 1. All hotels serve breakfast beginning at 6:00 a.m.
2. Hotel Phuket, Enchantment, and Tropicana serve lunch at 11:00 a.m.
3. All hotels serve dinner starting at 5:00 p.m.

Students can refer to the sample questions and answers shown below and table 1, which is shown below, to ask each other all kinds of questions.

This the worksheet where students can write down their questions or answers.

It is best to make several copies of this worksheet so students can practice this

activity many times.

RA:

CU:

RA:

CU:

RA:

CU:

RA:

CU:

RA:

CU:

RA:

CU:

RA:

CU:

RA:

CU:

RA:

CU:

RA:

CU:

RA:

CU:

RA:

Table 1. Information about Phuket's hotels and their services

Hotel	Tropicana		Enchantment		Trocs		Beach House		Hotel Phuket	
	Yes	No	Yes	No	Yes	No	Yes	No	Yes	No
Services										
Pool	X		X		X			X	X	
Nightclub	X		X		X			X		X
Restaurant	X		X					X		X
Airport Shuttle	X		X		X		X		X	
Mall Shuttle	X			X	X		X			X
Childcare	X		X		X			X		X
Room Service	X			X	X		X			X
Gym	X		X		X			X		X
Wi-Fi	X		X	X	X	X				
Spa	X		X		X			X		X
Meals Included	Yes	No	Yes	No	Yes	No	Yes	No	Yes	No
Breakfast	X		X		X		X		X	
Lunch	X		X		X		X		X	
Dinner	X		X		X			X		X
Buffet	X		X		X			X		X
Tours	X		X		X		X		X	
Krabi	X		X		X		X		X	
KataBeach	X		X		X		X		X	
PhiPhi	X		X		X		X		X	
Rentals										
BoatRental	X		X		X		X		X	
ScubaGear	X		X		X		X		X	
Motorcycle Rental	X		X		X			X		X
CarRental	X		X		X			X		X
Price Per Family Per Week	$ 2,400		$2,000		$1,600		$1,200		$1,000	

Hotel Reservation Answers

Is

Is there a scuba-diving area close to the hotel?
1. Yes, there is a scuba-diving area on the northeast side of the beach.
2. No, you must walk ten minutes to get to the scuba area.

Is there a quiet beach close to the hotel?
1. Yes, Kata Beach is a quiet beach, but you must take a taxi, car, or motorcycle to get there.

Is there a gym or an exercise area in the hotel?
1. Yes, there is a gym at the hotel.
2. No, there is no gym at your hotel, but you can go to some of the other hotels and pay to use their gym.

Is there a fruit and vegetable market close to the hotel?
1. Yes, there are fruits and vegetables for sale at the mall and for sale close to the hotels. There are also fruit stands on the south side of the beach.

Is there a nightclub area close to the hotel?
1. Yes, there are nightclubs in some of the hotels. If you are a guest at the hotel that has a nightclub, then there is no cover charge.
2. Yes, there is a nightclub area on the south side of the beach.
3. No, there is no nightclub at your hotel, but there are many nightclubs on the south side of the beach.

Is there a shuttle bus that can bring us to the mall or to the attractions?
1. Yes, some hotels have shuttle buses to bring their guests to the mall, or to some of the attractions, or to Kata Beach.
2. No, your hotel is very close to the mall, so you can easily walk to the mall.

Is the hotel on or close to the beach?
1. Yes, every hotel is close to or on the beach.

Is there a spa or massage services available at the hotel?
1. Yes, your hotel has spa and massage services. If you are a guest at the hotel, there is a discount.
2. No your hotel does not have a spa or massage service, but you caneasily go to a hotel that does and then pay to have those services.

Are

Are meals included in the price?
1. Yes, all meals are included at your hotel.
2. Yes, even the nightly buffet dinner is included at the hotel.
3. No, only breakfast and dinner are included in the price.
4. No, only breakfast is included at your hotel, but the hotel is close to
5. the mall and to many restaurants.

Are scuba rentals or boat rentals available at the hotel?
1. Yes, scuba rentals are available at the hotel.
2. No, but there are many places to rent scuba gear, and the rentals cost less at these places than at the other hotels.

Are tours included in the price?
1. Yes, you can take one free tour to Krabi, and there are unlimited rides to Kata Beach.

Are there day tours to Krabi?
1. Yes, there are, but the rent for a glass-bottom boat isn't included.
2. No, there are only free rides to Kata Beach.

Does

Does the hotel have twenty-four-hour room service?
1. Yes, your hotel has twenty-four-hour room service.
2. No, your hotel does not have twenty-four-hour room service.

Does the hotel offer childcare services?
1. Yes, your hotel has childcare services.
2. No, your hotel does not have childcare services.

Does the hotel have Wi-Fi?
1. Yes, all hotels have Wi-Fi.

Does the hotel have a swimming pool?
1. Yes, your hotel does have a swimming pool.
2. No, your hotel does not have a swimming pool.

Does my hotel offer scuba rentals?
1. Yes, your hotel offers scuba rentals.
2. No, your hotel does not offer scuba rentals, but many places all around the beach rent scuba gear, and at cheaper prices than hotels.

Does it cost extra to make local phone calls from the hotel room?

1. No, all hotels offer free local calls.

Do

Do the rooms have coffee, soft drinks, and a fridge?

1. Yes, all rooms in all the hotels have free tea and coffee, but it costs extra for soft drinks. All rooms have fridges as well.

What

What kind of food does the hotel serve?

1. All hotels serve Thai food, but the more expensive hotels serve the best Thai food.
1. All hotels serve Western style food.
2. There are many restaurants all around the beach as well.

What kind of activities take place at the hotel?

1. Hotel Phuket and the Tropicana offer free scuba lessons. These hotels also offer free dance lessons in the afternoon.
2. Your hotel has no free activities.

What time does the hotel serve the buffet dinner?

1. The hotels that serve the buffet dinner start serving at 5:00 p.m.

When

When is checkout?

1. Checkout on the last day of your stay is at noon.

When are the meals served?

1. All hotels serve breakfast beginning at 6:00 a.m.
1. Hotel Phuket, Enchantment, and the Tropicana serve lunch at 11:00 a.m.
2. All hotels serve dinner starting at 5:00 p.m.

When do the tours leave from the hotel?

1. A free bus to Kata Beach leaves on the hour, starting at 11:00 a.m.
2. The daily tour to Krabi leaves Hotel Phuket and the Tropicana at 9:00 a.m.

Who

Who owns the hotel?

1. Donald Trump
2. Connor
3. Tom

Where

<u>Where is Phuket?</u>
1. Phuket is an island in the southern part of Thailand.

<u>Where is the hotel located?</u>
1. Your hotel is right on the beach.
2. Your hotel is close to the beach.
3. Your hotel is a ten-minute walk to the beach.

Which

<u>Which is the better beach to swim at, Kata or Patong?</u>
1. Kata is much quieter and more peaceful.
2. Patong Beach is lively and has many shops and restaurants.

<u>Which side does my hotel room face, toward the beach or away from the beach?</u>
1. It depends on how much you pay. If you pay more, you can have a room that faces toward the beach.

How

<u>How far is the hotel from the shops or the mall?</u>
1. Hotel Phuket, Enchantment, and Tropicana are a ten- to fifteen-minute walk to the mall. These hotels have free shuttles to the mall, though.
2. Trocadero and Beach House are a few-minute walk to the mall.
3. Hotel Enchantment is right next to the mall.

<u>How much does the whole trip cost, including the plane fare?</u>
1. Airfare for each adult is $1,500, and $1,000 for each child under ten.
2. The cost of the hotel depends on which hotel you want to stay at.

<u>How many restaurants are there at the hotel?</u>
1. All hotels have at least one restaurant, but Enchantment and Tropicana have two restaurants, one that serves Thai meals and one that serves Western style food.

<u>How far is Kata Beach from Patong Beach?</u>
1. Kata Beach is about a twenty-minute ride from Patong Beach.

More Hotel Reservation Questions

Is

Is there a scuba-diving area close to the hotel?
Is there a quiet beach close to the hotel?
Is there a gym or an exercise area close to the hotel?
Is there a fruit and vegetable market close to the hotel?
Is there a nightclub area close to the hotel?
Is there a shuttle bus that can bring us to the mall or to the attractions?
Is the hotel on or close to the beach?
Is there a spa or massage service available at the hotel?

Are

Are meals included in the price?
Are scuba rentals or boat rentals available at the hotel?
Are tours included in the price?
Are there days tours to Krabi?
Are there any local festivals happening when we're in Thailand?

Does

Does the hotel have twenty-four-hour room service?
Does the hotel offer childcare services?
Does the hotel have Wi-Fi?
Does the hotel have a swimming pool?
Does it cost extra to make local phone calls from the hotel room?

Do

Do the rooms have coffee, soft drinks, and a fridge?

What

What kind of food does the hotel serve?
What kind of activities take place at the hotel?
What time does the hotel serve the buffet dinner?

When

When is checkout?
When are the meals served?
When do the tours leave from the hotel?

Who

Who owns the hotel?

Where

Where is Phuket?
Where is the hotel located?

Which

Which is the better beach to swim at, Kata or Patong?
Which side does my hotel room face, toward the beach or away from the beach?

How

How far is the hotel from the shops or the mall?
How much does the whole trip cost, including the plane fare?

How many restaurants are there at the hotel?
How far is Kata Beach from Patong Beach?

A11—Thai History

Present Perfect and Present Perfect Continuous

The verb tenses **present perfect** and **present perfect continuous** refer to actions that began in the past and that continue into the present.

Present Perfect: Refers to an action that began at an **indefinite** time in the past and that continues to the present.

I <u>have been working</u> at the power plant <u>for many years</u>.

The sentence **does not** reveal the number of years worked, but it does say that the person <u>began working</u> at this place <u>many years ago</u> and continues to do so.

Present Perfect Continuous: Refers to an action that began at a **definite** time in the past and that continues to the present.

(a)   I <u>have been working</u> at the power plant **for** <u>twenty years</u>.
(b)   I <u>have been working</u> at the power plant **since** <u>1995</u>.

Use   **for**   when using the **exact number of years** (or periods of time).
      since   when using the **exact year**.

Practice Exercises

(A)   Use the **present perfect.**

     1.   I have been studying at this school _____.
     2.   There's been less traffic in Bangkok _____ they built the subway.
     3.   I have lived in Chang Mai _____.
     4.   The Thais have been practicing Buddhism _____.

(B)   Use the **present perfect continuous.**

     1.   I have been studying at this school **for** _____.
     2.   I have been studying at this school **since** _____.
     3.   I have lived in Chang Mai **for** _____.
     4.   I have lived in Chang Mai **since** _____.

Main Exercise: In the following exercise, choose whether the sentence is present perfect (**PP**) or present perfect continuous (**PPC**).

1. __PPC__ King Bhumibol Adulyadej has been Thailand's king for sixty-eight years.

2. _____ Damnoen Saduak has been Thailand's busiest floating market for a long time.

3. _____ The story about Rama, which was first popularized in the south of Thailand in 400 BC, is still told today.

4. _____ Buddhism has been an important part of Thai life ever since the founding of the first Thai state.

5. _____ Monks have always had to follow a code of 277 rules.

6. _____ I have been visiting Wat Suan Dok every week for two months.

7. _____ Many Indians have been settling in Thailand since World War II.

8. _____ Chinese from China have been settling in Thailand for a long time.

9. _____ Chinese from the southeastern provinces of China have been settling in Thailand since the beginning of the nineteenth century.

10. _____ Ever since World War II, tribes from Burma continue to move into the hills and mountains of northern Thailand.

11. _____ Tribal life has always been distinguished by its reliance on nature.

12. _____ The use of ritual and the reliance on spirit doctors has been a main feature of Thai culture for a long time.

13. _____ Tina has been shopping in Bangkok's MBK (Ma Boon Krong) Centre for six hours now.

14. _____ The people of Ko Samui have relied on their coconut plantations for centuries.

15. _____ The main stone in Wat Phra Phuttabhat, which was discovered in 1623, is thought to carry magical powers that can heal a sick person.

16. _____ The West has influenced Thai culture and fashion for quite a while.

17. _____ Ever since the Ayuttyaha period of the seventeenth century, Thai artists have learned how to keep Buddhist manuscripts dry.

18. _____ Jim Thompson started his silk business in Thailand after World War II, and it still thrives to this day.

19. _____ The War Museum at the bridge on the River Kwai has been open ever since World War II ended.

20. _____ Ever since the abbot of Wat Pa Luanta Bua Yannasampanno adopted a tiger in 1999, the wat has become known as the Tiger Temple.

21. _____ Ever since they were built, the Bang Pa-In palace and its buildings have been regarded as one of the finest examples of Thai architecture.

22. _____ Even though the king abandoned his summer palace a few years after it was built in 1890, it still is a popular place for Thais to visit.

23. _____ Wat Kamphaeng, which marked the most southern spot of the Khmer empire in the twelfth century, is still a popular temple for Thais to visit.

24. Bangkok has been Thailand's capital since 1732.

25. _____ Thai people have enjoyed eating Western fast food for quite a while.

26. _____ The full-moon party, which began in Ko Phangan in the 1980s, is still one of the world's favorite parties for people from many countries.

27. _____ The elephant has been a symbol of Thailand for a long time.

28. _____ The evergreen rain forest in Khao Sok National Park is thought to be 160 million years old.

29. _____ The Chao Lay, Thailand's Sea Gypsy community, is the first indigenous community of Thais.

30. _____ Ko Ping Kan, or James Bond Island, has become famous ever since James Bond made a movie there.

31. _____ The dugong, a marine mammal sometimes known as a sea cow, has become an endangered species ever since people have hunted it for its meat, oil, skin, and bones.

32. _____ Taking a boat for transportation purposes on the Chao Praya River in Bangkok has been a common practice for centuries.

Thai Kings and Thai History

Place either **PP** or **PPC** in the spaces provided, depending on whether the underlined sentence is in the present perfect (**PP**) tense or present perfect continuous (**PPC**) tense.

(1) Thailand has a long, rich history, and much of that proud history is centered around its kings. As an example, the story about Rama, which was first popularized in the south of Thailand in 400 BC, is still told today. __**PPC**__ Kings are a big part of Thai life, but there are other symbols in Thailand that are also very important. The elephant, for example, has been a symbol of Thailand for a very long time. _____ The elephant is still an important symbol of Thailand, in the same way that the king will always be the most important Thai symbol.

(2) There are other important groups in Thai history as well. The Chao Lay, Thailand's Sea Gypsy community, was the first indigenous community of Thais. _____ Thailand began to grow as a nation after the Khmer empire started to decrease in power, starting in

the 1300s. King Ramkhaeng of Sukhothai began expanding his power southward in the eleventh century. The traditions laid by King Ramkhaeng have an important impact on Thai life, even to this day. _____ The king laid important foundations in art, politics, and literary traditions. King Ramkhaeng's society is thought of as the cradle of Thai civilization.

(3) The most important early civilization of Thailand, though, was the kingdom of Ayuttyaha, which was founded in the year 1350. _____ Only the rise of the Muslim state of Malacca in the fifteenth century prevented Ayuttyaha from extending its power all the way down the Malay peninsula. Cambodia might have also been added to the new Thai state if not for the contest wars against Chang Mai and Malacca. Siam did produce a very noble and popular king in the fourteenth century, King Borama Trailokanat, though. Trailokanat (1444–1488) _____ made important changes in the land regulatory system, as well as to his country's social and military administration. These changes lasted for several centuries, until the ascent of the great king, King Chulalongkorn, in the late nineteenth century. Chulalongkorn instituted a vast array of changes in Thai government and society, which last to this day. _____

(4) With the rise of the Burmese state in the fifteenth century, Thailand came under constant attack from Burma. It wasn't until 1590, when King Naresuan defeated the Burmese, _____ that the Thai state was allowed to be totally free from Burma. There was constant conflict between the Thai state and Europeans in the seventeenth and eighteenth centuries, but there was also conflict between Vietnam and Burma during these times. King Rama II became famous for reopening ties with the West in the early nineteenth century, and these ties remain to this day. _____ Although there were was some conflict with the French and the British, the Thai state kept its independence. The Burmese attack on Ayuttyaha in 1767 threatened Thailand and forced the movement of the Thai capital to Thonburi, just across the river from present-day Bangkok. Bangkok has therefore been the Thai capital ever since 1767. _____ General Phaya Takh Sin, who later became king, was the leader who held the Thai state together and established this new capital.

(5) There were many threats to Thailand during World War II, but the Thai state kept its independence. On December 16, 1946, Thailand joined the United Nations and has been a member ever since. _____ Thailand is also a vital member of SEATO, the Southeast Asian Treaty Organization, a group it joined many decades ago. _____ Thailand had an absolute monarchy for many centuries, but in 1932, a bloodless coup replaced the absolute monarchy with a constitutional, semiparliamentary monarchy. The military has therefore had a big influence on Thai politics, ever since 1932. _____

(6) King Bhumibol Adulyadej has been Thailand's king since 1946. _____ This king is an extremely popular king, and he is well loved by all Thais. Even though the king is the head of state, this king rarely interferes with the duties of politicians, unless, of course, their actions threaten the Thai state. King Bhumibal Adulyadej continues with many of the same traditions set by previous kings. The king has a number of residences in Thailand, but there are also places that he chooses not to live, such as the summer palace. The previous

king abandoned his summer palace a few years after it was built in 1890, but it still is a popular place for Thais to visit. _____ Thai people visit places like the summer palace because they love their kings, both present and past. Thais have placed great faith in their kings, all the way from King Ramkhaeng of Sukhothai in the fourteenth century, up to King Bhumibol Adulyadej, who still rules regally to this day. _____

A12—Motorcycles and Transportation in Thailand

Compound Words

A **hyphenated compound word** consists of two words, joined together by a hyphen. Guessing the meaning of a compound word is not always easy.

An example of a compound word is **chain-smoker**. If a person is a **chain-smoker**, then they smoke one cigarette after another, seemingly never being able to stop smoking. The word chain in the compound word implies that the cigarettes are linked together like the links in a chain. The links in a chain come one after the other, and the links are joined together. So for the smoker, the cigarettes smoked are linked together in a chain, because this person cannot seem to stop smoking.

Another compound word is **tree-hugger**. It is not so easy to guess the meaning of this compound word, but it means environmentalist. A tree hugger loves nature, and so do environmentalists. This person naturally loves trees: so the term **tree-hugger**.

Regular compound words like **cupboard** or **handbag** are in the dictionary and are not joined together by a hyphen.

Here are other examples of hyphenated compound words and their meanings:

Compound Word	Meaning
all-nighter	usually refers to when a person stays up and studies all night before an important test
couch potato	a person who is lazy and who usually just sits on couch and watches TV
early bird	a person who wakes up early in the morning
gas-guzzler	a car that uses a lot of gas and is not fuel efficient
go-getter	an aggressive, motivated individual
night-owl	a person who stays up late and loves the night
penny-pincher	a miserly person who does not like to spend money
rabble-rouser	usually refers to a person who is a troublemaker
team-player	an unselfish person who works well with others
well-read	an educated, worldly individual who reads a lot
well-spoken	a person who speaks well, eloquently, and who has a good grasp of the facts

Practice: Take a compound word from above and make a sentence out of it.

<u>Example</u>:   Tina is a real **go-getter**. She has two jobs and already has her house paid off.

1. _____.

2. _____.

The story on the next page has many compound words. Before reading it, try your best to figure out what each compound word means. The aim of this lesson is to use your logic to figure out the meanings of the compound words. Refer to the story for help. Some of the compound words listed below are not hyphenated.

motor scooters   _____

fuel-efficient   <u>refers to a motorcycle or car that does not use much gas</u>

multifaceted   _____

well-to-do   <u>refers to a person who is rich and has a lot of money</u>

heavily congested   _____

often-seen   _____

overrun   _____

danger-prone   _____

breastfeed   _____

taxi-men   _____

low-cost   <u>something that does not cost a lot of money to operate or buy</u>

well marked   _____

well defined   _____

cycle-propelled   _____

people-powered   _____

run-down,   _____

out-of-date   _____

awe-inspiring   _____

premodern   _____

elephant trekking _____

self-propelled   <u>a vehicle that is not powered by a motor but that is powered by a person,</u>
                  <u>such as a bicycle</u>

must-see   _____

meat eaters   _____

well-known   _____

engine-powered   _____

odd-looking   _____

well built   _____

third-class   _____

first-class   _____

Story—Motorcycles and Transportation in Thailand

Some of the most interesting things to observe in Thailand are the **motor scooters** and the people that ride them. Even though there are many motor scooters in Taiwan, there are many, many more in Thailand. I saw some odd passenger arrangements on the motor scooters in Taiwan, like a woman riding a motor scooter with a small baby in each hand, but the passenger arrangements on the motor scooters in Thailand are much more interesting. Motorcycles and motor scooters offer **fuel-efficient** travel options, because they do not use as much gas as cars do. Motorcycles and motor scooters are just one of the important cogs in the **multifaceted** Thai transportation system.

The most interesting passenger arrangement I saw in Thailand was when seven people were on one motorcycle: Yes, there were seven people on one motorcycle! Motorcycles that carry four, five, or six passengers are a very common sight in Bangkok. The more **well-to-do** of Bangkok's residents do not use motorcycles, but many ordinary Thais do. Even though Bangkok is the biggest city in Thailand, there are also many motorcycle and motor scooter riders in smaller Thai cities. Nothing, though, can match the sheer number and the interesting arrangements of motorcycles or riders in Bangkok. Since Bangkok is a **heavily congested** city with lots of traffic, motorcycles serve a very important transportation function there.

The use of motorcycle is also an **often-seen** phenomenon in other countries in Southeast Asia. Vietnam's capital city, Ho Chi Minh City, is practically **overrun** with motor scooters. When I went to Phnom Penh in Cambodia, I took a motorcycle into the city from the airport. When we stopped at a traffic light, I took a picture of four people that were sitting on a motorcycle next to me (figure 1). There were motorcycles or motor scooters throughout Phnom Penh, but the drivers make riding on a motorcycle or motor scooter a very **danger-prone** experience, because the drivers very often do not obey traffic signals or traffic signs.

Whole families sometimes ride on a motorcycle, as shown in figure 2 (page 251). In this photo, the father is steering the motorcycle while the mother sits in the back to make sure that none of her children fall off. The photo also shows how children sometimes ride in the front of the motorcycle, right in front of the driver, but this does not seem to be a very safe practice. Mothers sometimes feed or even **breastfeed** their child when they are riding on the backseat of a motorcycle.

Motorcycles serve a very important function in Thailand's transportation system. In Bangkok, for example, many motorcycle taxis are available for hire throughout the city. The **taxi-men** wear brightly colored orange vests, so it is easy to spot them. Taking a ride on one of these motorcycle taxis is a very **low-cost** way of getting around. Since the motorcycle taxis are quite small, they can easily maneuver through the big traffic jams in Bangkok. There are often special motorcycle lanes on Bangkok's streets as well, so this makes it quite easy to get around town on a motorcycle. All motorcycle lanes are **well marked** and **well defined**, so this makes it safer for motorcycle riders to get around.

Tourists can also easily rent motorcycles in beach areas like Phuket. All that is needed is a passport and a cash deposit, and anyone of age can rent a motorcycle. It is very convenient to rent a motorcycle in places like Phuket, because it is quite a big island, and there are many different beaches to see or visit.

Cycle-driven carriages are also available for those people who are not in a rush, and this **people-powered** form of transportation provides good exercise and a source of income for many Thais. Some of the older carriages look quite **run-down**, but they are still charming and safe to ride on. Of course, elephants can also serve as forms of transportation, for those who want to get out of the city and into the countryside to use this now **out-of-date** form of transportation. Riding on an elephant can be quite **awe-inspiring**, as they are very powerful yet gentle animals. Elephants are one of the symbols of Thailand, but in **premodern** days, elephants did a lot of work in the jungles. These days, there are many elephant safaris available for any person who wants to go **elephant trekking**.

Getting around by boat is also a form of transportation in Bangkok, and there are many boats that provide passenger services for those who may need to cross one of Bangkok's rivers.

There are also a number of floating markets in Thailand where tourists and local Thais alike can float down a river and shop at any of the market stalls along the river. The boats are not **self-propelled**; they are often paddled by older women who wear colorful clothes and hats, so a trip to the floating market is a **must-see** in Thailand. The markets sell mostly fruits and vegetables, so they may not be a favorite spot for **meat eaters**. The floating markets are one of Thailand's most **well-known** attractions.

Getting around a Thai city is also made easier by vehicles called tuk-tuks. The tuk-tuks are small **engine-powered** vehicles that are smaller than a car and can maneuver easily in Bangkok's traffic. These **odd-looking** vehicles are a favorite of tourists, but they are also used by local Thais. The tuk-tuks seem to be very **well built**, so it is not dangerous to ride on them.

One of my favorite ways to get around Thailand when I lived there was to ride the **third-class** trains. This is truly a **low-cost** alternative to **first-class** travel, and it is also a lot more fun. Thailand therefore offers myriad choices of travel and transportation options for tourists who want to experience something different.

Directions: Answer the following questions with at least one sentence.

1. If you had a choice, and if you lived in Thailand, which job would you rather have, a taxi-man on a motor scooter or a tuk-tuk operator?

2. If you lived in Thailand, would you not be afraid to ride on a motorcycle or a motor scooter with many people on it? Why or why not?

3. Have you noticed many gas-guzzlers in the city where you live? Should the government outlaw gas-guzzlers?

4. In some movies, passengers ride on top of trains. In some countries, some passengers also ride on the top of buses. Do you think this is too dangerous, and should it be outlawed?

5. In cities like Bangkok, boats are often used as a form of transportation. Riding on a boat to work or to school can be a lot of fun. Would you ride to work or to school on a boat?

6. Draw one of the following pictures:
   (a) you and your friends riding together on one motorcycle
   (b) you and a friend riding in a tuk-tuk

A13—Thai Marine Life

Adjectives—Order of Importance

An adjective is a word that describes a noun or a pronoun.

Adjectives have degrees of importance: they are ordered in terms of importance when describing nouns or pronouns.

Order of Adjectives:

1. <u>Determiners</u>   a, an, for, her, his, their, your, the
2. <u>Size and shape</u>   big, small
3. <u>Observation</u>   beautiful
4. <u>Age</u>   old, young, new
5. <u>Color</u>   blue
6. <u>Origin</u>   Canadian
7. <u>Material</u>   wooden, paper
8. <u>Qualifier</u>   touring

Examples:

Jim was driving <u>the</u> <u>beautiful</u>, <u>big</u>, <u>old</u>, <u>red</u>, <u>Italian</u> sports car.
                  1   2   3   4   5   6

Prim is eating with <u>a</u> <u>small</u>, <u>old</u>, <u>wooden</u> spoon.
                   1   3   4   7

Pugsley is <u>an</u> <u>attractive</u>, <u>small</u>, <u>young</u>, <u>white</u> dog.
          1   2   3   4   5

Thailand is <u>a</u> <u>beautiful</u>, <u>big</u>, <u>ancient</u> country.
          1   2   3   4

Prang works for <u>a</u> <u>big</u>, <u>new</u>, <u>international</u> company.
          1 3   4   6

Thai Marine Life

There are many beautiful, tropical species of marine life in Thai waters. Make sentences with these types of marine life, with emphasis on order of importance.

clownfish   puffer fish   crown of thorns starfish

dugong   scorpion fish   bottlenose dolphin

lagoon triggerfish

Use **adjectives** to write sentences about Thai marine life.

Example:

1.   (a)   The clownfish is <u>a</u> <u>beautiful</u>, <u>small</u> fish.
                                  1   2   3

      (b)   The clownfish is <u>an</u> <u>exotic-looking</u>, <u>small</u>, <u>striped</u> fish.
                                   1   2   3   5

      (c)   The clownfish is <u>a</u> <u>strange-looking</u>, <u>striped</u>, <u>Thai</u> fish.
                                  1   2   5   6

      (d)   The clownfish is <u>an</u> <u>orange-faced</u> fish.
                                   1   2

   (a)–(d)   The clownfish is <u>a</u> <u>beautiful, exotic, and strange-looking</u>, <u>orange-</u>
                                  1   2   2   2   2

          <u>faced</u>, <u>small</u>, <u>striped</u>, <u>Thai</u> fish.
             3   5   6

Now write a few of your own sentences about the clownfish:

(e) _____

(f) _____

The two tables of adjectives will help you describe Thai marine life:

Determiner 1	Size and Shape 2	Observation 3	Age 4
a	big	beautiful	young
an	huge	pretty	old
for	large	gorgeous	new
the	humungous	attractive	
	great	good-looking	
	sizeable	handsome	
	small	ravishing	
	tiny	shiny	
	little	glowing	
	round	ugly	
	oblong	horrid	
	square	hideous	
	oval	unsightly	
	triangular	exotic-looking	

Color 5	Origin 6	Material 7	Qualifier 8
blue	Thai	wooden	
red	Canadian	metal	
orange	American	paper	
yellow	British	glass	
purple	Brazilian	human-skinned	
striped	Italian	animal-skinned	
gray, grayish	Asian	fish-skinned	
brightly colored	European	spiny	
dull	international	pointy	

bright			
opaque			
silvery			
golden			

Special Adjectives

herbivorous	- to feed on plants, plant matter, or vegetables (dugong)
carnivorous	- to feed on meat, fish, or flesh
mammalian	- a mammal
svelte	- slim, slender, slippery
cetacean	- dugongs are mammals, dolphins are cetaceans
cetaceous	- word used to describe a cetacean
poisonous	- these types of fish are dangerous to touch (scorpion fish)
lateral	- on the side (The cuttlefish has lateral fins.)

Directions: For each species, write descriptive sentences with adjectives (in proper order) from the table of adjectives above. You can also use any other adjective.

1.   The Puffer Fish

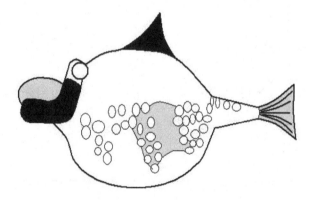

Example: The puffer fish puffs itself up so it can have <u>a</u> <u>big</u>, <u>round</u> belly.
                                                                    1   2   3

(a) <u>The puffer fish is a</u> _____

(b) _____

(c) _____

2. Crown of Thorns Starfish

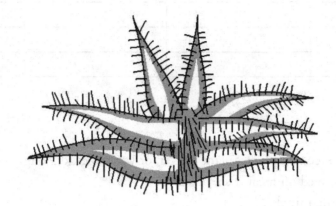

(a) _____

(b) _____

(c) _____

3. The Dugong

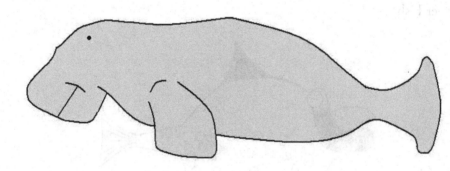

(a) _____

(b) _____

(c) _____

4. Bottlenose Dolphin

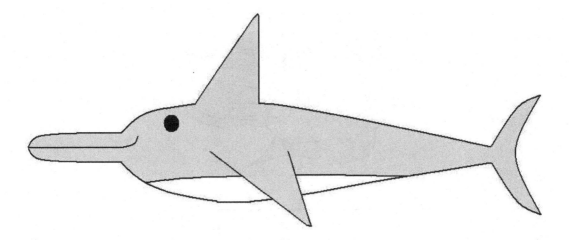

(a) _____

(b) _____

(c) _____

5. Scorpion Fish

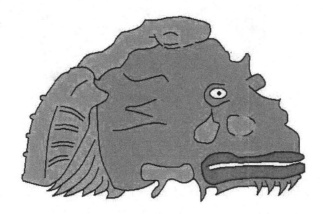

(a) _____

(b) _____

(c) _____

6.   The Cuttlefish

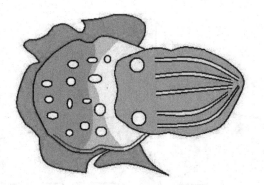

(a) _____

(b) _____

(c) _____

7.   The Lagoon Triggerfish

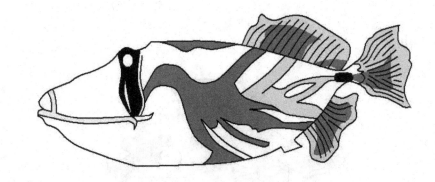

(a) _____

(b) _____

(c) _____

(d) _____

(e) _____

A14—Thailand's Mountains and Caves

Descriptive Writing with Slang, Phrasal Verbs, and Idiomatic Phrases

The story "Thai Mountains and Caves" contains many new words. Match the words with their definitions. This is probably best done by splitting the class up into groups and having each group define a particular set of words. Then discuss the words in class. Then students will read the story fully by themselves.

Directions: Match the phrases with their meanings.

Nouns, Verbs, Adverbs, and Adjectives

1.	advent	_(c)_	(a)	the most important or the greatest
2.	previously hidden	_____	(b)	a modern, popular, or new way of doing something, or a new fashion
3.	popular trend	_____	(c)	the coming or the arrival of something important
4.	most prominent	_(a)_	(d)	something that was hidden or that was previously undiscovered
5.	wonders of nature	_____	(e)	refers to statues that are put in caves, making the inside of the caves more beautiful
6.	replicas of Thai	_____	(f)	refers to beauties of nature
7.	adorn this cave	_____	(g)	copies or models of Thai wats

Phrasal Verbs (Review appendix A, phrasal verbs, if needed.)

1.	lay unspoiled	_(g)_	(a)	occurs when many people visit a place to take part in an activity
2.	straddled along	_____	(b)	to pay respect to
3.	sawed down	_____	(c)	to preside over, to have power over, to be the king or queen of
4.	opened up	_____	(d)	situated or placed along something
	opening up		(e)	to have many things bunched together in a geographical area
5.	ruled over	_____	(f)	watch an event, ceremony, or game

6. flocking to   (g) refers to large parts of land or large parts of a country that have not been used or destroyed by humans

7. dotted with   _____   (h) to be cut down with a saw
   dotted them

8. pay reverence to   _____   (i) exposed or revealed for the first time

9. take in this   _____

Idiomatic Phrases

1. hugged the coastline _____ (a) wonderful things built by humans

2. buzz of loggers' _____ (b) bathing in waterfalls represents a search for balance between two different ways of life
   chainsaws

3. drew a line in the sand __l__ (c) in a position close to the coast

4. Buddhism was brought _____ (d) the noise made by the chainsaws of loggers
   to the Thai hilltops

5. human-inspired _____ (e) refers to beautiful, natural things on the tops of hills
   wonders

6. acknowledged the _____ (f) refers to things done to bring the Buddhist religion to people who lived on the hills
   power of the mountains

7. paying homage to _____ (g) refers to the calm and peace people feel when practicing the Buddhist religion
   and appeasing the
   mountain gods

8. adorning its hilltop _____ (h) refers to the dual nature of the waterfalls and how they can represent both the fast pace of modern city life and the serene peace of Buddhism are created by people

9. hectic pace of modern _____ (i) to show respect to the power of gods in the mountains
   city life

10. the peace and serenity _____ (j) refers to the fast pace of city life
    of Buddhism

11. symbolic of the polar __h__ (k) recognizing that mountains have spiritual or mystical powers
    nature of modern life

12. search for a balance _____ (l) - take a stand against something
    between these two   - to set limits, so as to prevent damaging
    contending opposites   something even more

Thai Mountains and Caves

Directions: Answer the questions after reading the story.

(1) One hundred years ago, more than 90 percent of Thailand's mountains and forests **lay unspoiled**. Thai cities either **hugged the coastline** or were **straddled along** the rivers on the Thai plains. With the **advent** of the automobile, and with the **buzz of loggers' chainsaws**, the Thai mountain wilderness was **opened up**, or **sawed down**, and made available for Thai people. Thais began visiting and then populating **previously hidden** forested areas.

(2) Some bad things came from these changes, but there were also some very good things. The **opening up** of Thailand's interior created problems for the survival of Thailand's wilderness areas, so the government created Thailand's first national park, Khao Yai, in 1961. By 2000, Thailand had fifty national parks, ensuring that Thailand's forest, jungles, and wildlife would be protected. The Thai government **drew a line in the sand** fifty years ago, and because of this, Thailand's national parks are flourishing.

(3) When the mountainous jungle areas were **opened up**, Thais naturally **flocked** to these areas. Temples were built on mountaintops, and cities and towns sprouted up on the mountains, which brought **Buddhism to the Thai hilltops**. With the movement of people into the mountains and jungles, many **wonders of nature** were discovered, but many **human-inspired wonders were also given life**.

(4) Thais knew their coastlines and coastal islands were **dotted with** caves, but many more caves were later discovered in Thailand's mountains. Thai kings eventually started to **pay reverence to** the mountains and to the special powers that lie deep within them and their caves. King Indraditya, who **ruled over** Sukhothai centuries ago, **acknowledged the power of the mountains** by **paying homage to and appeasing** the mountain god in his religious ceremonies. Thais began building their temples (wats) on mountaintops, and they also began placing Buddha statues at the mouths of mountain caves. Soon after that, shrines were built inside caves, the **most prominent** being the Khao Banda-it shrine inside a cave in Petchaburi.

(5) The Khao Banda-it shrine has a very large Buddha statue inside it, but there is much more inside it. Many smaller Buddha statues **adorn this cave**, as do **replicas of Thai wats**. Religious ceremonies are held many times a day inside caves like this, and many Thais pay homage to Buddha in them. Dai Inthanon, Thailand's tallest mountain peak, also has a huge wat **adorning its hilltop**. Water and rivers flow through the Thai mountains, so there are many waterfalls **dotting them**. King Chulalongkorn (Rama IV) started a **popular trend** by bathing in the pool of water below Sai Yok waterfall in Kanchanaburi provinces. Now, many Thais **take in this popular pastime** by **flocking to** and bathing in Thailand's many waterfalls.

(6) The splashing waters of the waterfalls, which represent the **hectic pace of modern city life**, and the quiet, serene pools of water that accumulate at the base of the waterfalls, which represent **the peace and serenity of Buddhism**, are **symbolic of the polar nature of modern**

life. The now-common practice of bathing in Thailand's waterfalls represents the **search for a balance between these two contending opposites**.

Writing or Speaking Exercises

Directions: Discuss the questions as a class or in groups, or write down the answers.

1. In paragraph 1, what does the phrase **hugged the coastline** refer to?
   (a) Someone hugged the people who lived on the coastline.
   (b) Thai cites only hugged the coastline.
   (c) Thai cities that were built on the coast.
   (d) People who lived on the coastline liked to hug each other.
   (e) None of the above.

2. In your words, describe what this phrase in paragraph 2 means: "The Thai government **drew a line in the sand** fifty years ago ..."

3. Paragraph 5: How are **adorning its hilltop** and **dotting them** similar?

4. Paragraph 3 talks about **wonders of nature** and **human-inspired wonders**. What is the difference between these two kinds of wonders?

5. In paragraph 4, what does the phrase **most prominent** mean?
   (a) the best
   (b) the most well known
   (c) the biggest
   (d) the longest
   (e) the most beautiful

6. From paragraph 6, discuss how Thai waterfalls represent the **balance** that Thai people **search for in their lives**.

7. In paragraph 4, what does **pay reverence to the mountain** mean?
   (a) Pay money, so the mountain doesn't become a volcano.
   (b) Keep the mountain god happy so that it won't get angry.
   (c) The mountain likes money.
   (d) The mountain is powerful, so the king had to give it money.
   (e) Pay respect to the mountain and to the spirit of the mountain.

8. **Adorn** is used twice in paragraph 5: **adorning its hilltop, adorn this cave**. In your own words, describe what **adorn** means in both cases.

9. In paragraph 1, what does the phrase **previously hidden** mean?

Appendix A

Two-Part Phrasal Verbs

Many verbs in English are followed by an adverb or a preposition (also called a particle). These are called two-part verbs, or phrasal verbs. The particle that follows the verb sometimes changes the meaning of the phrasal verb.

Phrasal Verb	Meaning	Example
drop off	decline gradually	The hill dropped off near the river.
drop off (2)	to fall asleep	While watching TV, he dropped off.
drop off (3)	give something to someone	Would you drop this package off at the front desk?

Types of Phrasal Verbs

separable   – The particle **can** be separated from the verb.
inseparable   – The particle **cannot** be separated from the verb.
intransitive   – The phrasal verb **cannot** take a direct object.

Separable	add up (means to add)	Correct: She added up the total on her calculator.
		Correct: She added the total up on her calculator.
Inseparable	get around (means to evade)	Correct: She always gets around the rules.
		Incorrect: She always gets the rules around. (This makes no sense.)
Intransitive	catch on (means to understand)	Correct: After I explained the math problem, she began to catch on.
		Incorrect: She began to catch on the math problem. ("catch on" cannot take a direct object)

Unfortunately, there is no way to know whether a phrasal verb is separable, inseparable, or intransitive. In most cases, phrasal verbs must be memorized.

Free Phrasal Verb Exercises or Lessons on the Internet:

http://www.englishpage.com/prepositions/prepositions.html
https://www.realenglishconversations.com/english-phrasal-verbs-podcast-free/
https://www.realenglishconversations.com/do-up-1english-phrasal-verb-lesson/
http://www.oxfordonlineenglish.com/free-phrasal-verb-lessons
http://www.teach-this.com/resources/activities/phrasal-verbs
http://www.teach-this.com/images/resources/acting-out.pdf
http://englishexpressyes.com/free-english-phrasal-verb-tutoring-videos.html
www.youtube.com → search for phrasal verbs

Online Courses for General English:

https://www.universalclass.com/i/course/writing-basics-101.htm?gclid=CPmkusn90c8CFQ9xfgod_l4Jqg

Free Lists of Meanings of Phrasal Verbs:

https://www.englishclub.com/vocabulary/phrasal-verbs-list.htm
http://grammar.ccc.commnet.edu/grammar/phrasals.htm
https://www.usingenglish.com/reference/phrasal-verbs/list.html
http://www.englishpage.com/prepositions/phrasaldictionary.html
https://www.easypacelearning.com/all-lessons/grammar/1219-phrasal-verbs-list-meanings-and-examples

Appendix B

List of Prepositions

The prepositions **of**, **to**, and **in** are among the ten most frequently used words in English. This is a short list of seventy of the more common prepositions.

- about   above   across   after   at   as
- against   along   amid   among   around
- before   behind   below   beneath   beside
- beside   between   beyond   but   by
- concerning   considering
- despite   down   during
- except   excepting   excluding
- following   for   from
- inside   into   in
- like
- minus
- near   nearby
- off   on   onto   opposite   outside   over
- past   per   plus
- regarding   round
- save   since
- than   through   to   toward
- under   unlike   until   underneath   up   upon
- versus   via
- with   within   without

Lists of Prepositions:

https://www.englishclub.com/grammar/prepositions-list.htm
https://www.englishclub.com/vocabulary/prepositions/list.htm
https://en.wikipedia.org/wiki/List_of_English_prepositions
http://www.english-grammar-revolution.com/list-of-prepositions.html
http://grammar.yourdictionary.com/parts-of-speech/prepositions/list-of-common-prepositions.html

Appendix C

From Lesson A12: Definitions of Compound Words

motor scooters	a small motorcycle
fuel-efficient	motorcycle or car that does not use much gas
multifaceted	something that has many uses or many functions (As an example: My cell phone is multifaceted. I can use it to make phone calls, send faxes, and send e-mails.)
well-to-do	refers to a person who is rich and has a lot of money
heavily congested	refers to the streets of Bangkok, which are filled with cars
often-seen	something that is easily visible or easy to see
overrun	far too much of something
danger prone	something that is risky and dangerous
breastfeed	refers to how a woman naturally feeds her baby
taxi-men	men who operate motorcycle taxis in Bangkok
low-cost	something that does not cost a lot of money to operate or buy
well-marked	something that is easy to see and that is not hidden
well-defined	something that is easy to understand or notice
cycle-driven	a bicycle type vehicle that is operated and powered by a person
people-powered	something, like a bicycle, that is powered by a person

run-down	old, not usable anymore, torn apart, broken
out-of-date	old-fashioned, something that is not used anymore
awe-inspiring	something that is so wonderful and so great that it is so awesome
premodern	a thing, like a carriage powered by horses, that is not used in these modern times
elephant trekking	to ride an elephant on a long journey
self-propelled	a vehicle that is not powered by a motor but that is powered by a person, such as a bicycle
must-see	something that is so terrific that you cannot miss seeing it
meat eaters	animals or people that eat meat
well-known	famous, known to many people
engine-powered	a vehicle that gets its power from a motor or an engine
odd-looking	strange, strange appearance, odd look, strange look
well built	sturdy, stable, built well, will last a long time, will work well
third-class	the least expensive, not the best
first-class	the best, the most expensive

Appendix D

List of Irregular Verbs

http://www.englishpage.com/irregularverbs/irregularverbs.html
http://speakspeak.com/resources/vocabulary-general-english/english-irregular-verbs
https://www.englishclub.com/vocabulary/irregular-verbs-list.htm
https://www.ego4u.com/en/cram-up/grammar/irregular-verbs
https://ca.images.search.yahoo.com/search/images;_ylt=AwrSbjZzefxXoGUAJZ7rFAx.;_ylu=X
3oDMTEyaW5yanVtBGNvbG8DZ3ExBHBvcwMxBHZ0aWQDQjAzMDlfMQRzZWMD
c2M-?p=List+of+Irregular+Verbs&slotting=yst&fr=yfp-t-CA006%2CCA203

Appendix E

Information for Wh Questions

(a) http://dictionary.cambridge.org/dictionary/english/wh-question

wh- question   noun [C]

/dʌb.əl.juːˈeɪtʃ ˌkwes.tʃən/ /dʌb.əl.juːˈeɪtʃ ˌkwes.tʃən/ specialized

a **question** in **English** that is a **request** for **information**. Wh- **questions** usually **start** with a word **beginning** with wh-, but "how" is also **included**. The wh- words are: what, when, where, who, whom, which, whose, why and how.

(b) https://www.englishclub.com/vocabulary/wh-question-words.htm

WH Question Words

We use question words to ask certain types of questions. We often refer to these words as *WH words* because they include the letters *WH* (for example *WH*y, *H*o*W*).

(c) www.englishclub.com/vocabulary/wh-question-words.htm

Questions: *wh*-questions

from English Grammar Today

Wh-questions begin with *what, when, where, who, whom, which, whose, why* and *how*. We use them to ask for information. The answer cannot be *yes* or *no*:

A: ***When*** *do you finish college?*   *Next year.*
B: ***Who*** *is your favourite actor?*   *George Clooney for sure!*

(d) https://www.ecenglish.com/learnenglish/how-use-wh-questions

In English there are seven 'Wh…' questions. Here's what they are and how they are used:

What: used for a thing.

'What is it?'

Who: used for a person. <u>Whose</u> has the same meaning. It is always followed by a noun.

'Who were you talking to?'   *'Whose car is that?'*

Why: used for a reason.

'Why were you late?'

When: used for a time or date

'When did you start working here?'

Which: used for a choice.

'Which do you prefer, tea or coffee?'

Where: used for a place.

'Where do you live?'

How: used for an amount, or the way.

'How much does it cost?'   *'How do I get to the station?'*

B1
1.	J	2.	D	3.	E	4.	I	5.	C
6.	B	7.	F	8.	G	9.	A	10.	H
11.	K								
1.	D	2.	G	3.	F	4.	C	5.	A
6.	B	7.	I	8.	H	9.	E		
1.	F	2.	B	3.	H	4.	E	5.	A
6.	C	7.	D	8.	G				
1.	3	2.	3	3.	2	4.	6	5.	1 1/2
6.	3	7.	1/2	8.	4	9.	13	10.	3
1.	6	2.	1	3.	3	4.	10	5.	6 1/2
6.	1	7.	1/2	8.	4	9.	13	10.	3
1.	2	2.	5 1/2	3.	11	4.	4 1/2		
5.	1	6.	2 1/2	7.	1 1/2	8.	2		
9.	2	10.	1 1/2	11.	1				

B2
1.	beautiful	2.	delicious	3.	striped
4.	sour	5.	big	6.	clear
7.	tasty	8.	hot	9.	pointy
10.	large				

1. Puffer Fish
1. The puffer fish is spotted.
2. The puffer fish can be round when it puffs itself up.
3. The puffer fish has a black fin.
4. The puffer fish has a funny face.
5. The puffer fish has gray nose.

2. Crown of Thorns Starfish
1. The crown of thorns starfish is spiky.
2. The crown of thorns starfish has many legs (arms).
3. The crown of thorns starfish has long legs (arms).
4. The crown of thorns starfish is partly pink and partly white.
5. The crown of thorns starfish is exotic-looking.

3. Dugong
1. The dugong is fat.
2. The dugong has a big stomach.
3. The dugong has a hammer-like jaw.
4. The dugong has a round head.
5. The dugong has a big body.

4. Bottlenose Dolphin

1. The bottlenose dolphin has a <u>long</u> snout (nose).
2. The bottlenose dolphin has a <u>slim</u> body.
3. The bottlenose dolphin has a <u>happy</u> smile.
4. The bottlenose dolphin is a <u>good</u> swimmer.
5. The bottlenose dolphin has <u>two</u> flippers.

5. Scorpion Fish

1. The scorpion fish has a <u>mean</u> face.
2. The scorpion fish has an <u>orange</u> body.
3. The scorpion fish has <u>red</u> lips.
4. The scorpion fish's body is partly <u>pink</u>.
5. The scorpion fish has <u>rough</u> skin.

6. Cuttlefish

1. The cuttlefish has an <u>oval</u> head.
2. The cuttlefish has <u>yellow</u> lines on its face.
3. The cuttlefish has a <u>blue</u> and <u>purple</u> body.
4. The cuttlefish has <u>white</u> spots on its body.
5. The cuttlefish has <u>no</u> arms.

7. Lagoon Triggerfish

1. The lagoon triggerfish has a <u>long</u> body.
2. The lagoon triggerfish has <u>yellow</u> lines on its face.
3. The lagoon triggerfish has <u>two</u> fins.
4. The lagoon triggerfish has a <u>long</u> face.
5. The lagoon triggerfish has <u>gray</u> patterns on its body.

B3 **Practice Exercises**

1. mine	2. she's	3. me, yours	4. mine, yours	5. her
6. they	7. we	8. I, my	9. we	10. my, her

Main Exercises

1. his, he	2. they, they	3. I, he we	4. he, I, I
5. I., I, I	6. he, he, we, we	7. they, they, they	8. she, her, she
9. I, he, he, he	10. I, he, we	11. my, my, she	12. my, his, he
13. my, my, she, my, he			

B4 **Practice Exercise**

1. biggest	2. more expensive	3. taller
4. taller	5. highest	6. most popular
7. bigger	8. the finest	9. the hottest

10. the highest 11. the most diverse 12. the largest
13. the most enchanting 14. the tallest 15. the most popular
16. spiciest 17. earliest 18. the most fun
19. noisiest 20. the most brilliant

Main Exercise

1. smaller
2. biggest
3. smallest
4. most interesting
5. the most interesting
6. bigger
7. biggest
8. the most colorful
9. highest
10. smallest
11. smaller
12. biggest
13. smaller
14. the most intelligent
15. smaller
16. the most powerful
17. Bigger
18. the most powerful
19. smaller
20. heavier
21. higher
22. smallest
23. bigger, heavier
24. the most extraordinary
25. the most dangerous
26. Lower
27. the most immovable
28. more flexible
29. more pointy
30. the shortest
31. heavier
32. faster

B5 **Practice Exercises**

1. teeth 2. turtles 3. feet 4. tails 5. shrimp
6. beaches 7. eyes 8. Fish 9. toes 10. waves
11. sand 12. drinks

Main Exercise

1. teeth 2. snouts 3. fish 4. feet
5. arms 6. necks 7. gills 8. shells
9. women 10. legs 11. schools 12. predators
13. octopi 14. shells 15. shelves 16. bellies
17. coral reefs 18. algae 19. shrimp 20. beaches
21. water 22. tears 23. lives 24. blood
25. leaves 26. stripes

B6 **Main Exercise**

1. Fish	The fish is	**under**	the shark.
	The fish is	**above**	the dolphin.
	The fish is	**next to**	the turtle.
2. Dugong	The dugong is	**next to**	the mermaid.
	The dugong is	**above**	the clownfish.
	The dugong is	**on top of**	the turtle.

3. <u>Mermaid</u>   The mermaid is   **next to**   the dugong.

                The mermaid is   **above**   the clownfish.

                The mermaid is   **above**   the turtle.

4. <u>Dolphin</u>   The dolphin is   **next to**   the turtle.

                The dolphin is   **under**   the shark.

                The dolphin is   **above**   the swordfish.

5. <u>Turtle</u>   The turtle is   **next to**   the dolphin.

                The turtle is   **above**   the clownfish.

                The turtle is   **under**   the dugong.

6. <u>Swordfish</u>   The swordfish is   **next to**   the clownfish.

                The swordfish is   **under**   the shark.

                The swordfish is   **below**   the dolphin.

7. <u>Clownfish</u>   The clownfish is   **under**   the turtle.

                The clownfish is   **next to**   the swordfish.

                The clownfish is   **under**   the dugong.

B7   **Practice Exercise**

<u>1.</u> I'm   <u>2.</u> I'll   <u>3.</u> they've   <u>4.</u> she's

<u>5.</u> they'll   <u>6.</u> she's   <u>7.</u> he's   <u>8.</u> Jobim's

<u>9.</u> Jobim'll   <u>10.</u> he's   <u>11.</u> he's   <u>12.</u> they're

<u>13.</u> they've

Main Exercise

<u>1.</u> I'm   <u>2.</u> she's   <u>3.</u> we're   <u>4.</u> I've

<u>5.</u> we're   <u>6.</u> we'll, weren't   <u>7.</u> we'll, isn't   <u>8.</u> It's

<u>9.</u> she's   <u>10.</u> let's   <u>11.</u> they're   <u>12.</u> they've

<u>13.</u> it's   <u>14.</u> they're   <u>15.</u> It's   <u>16.</u> fruit's, it's, isn't

<u>17.</u> aren't   <u>18.</u> isn't   <u>19.</u> we'll   <u>20.</u> we're

<u>21.</u> It's   <u>22.</u> they're   <u>23.</u> It's   <u>24.</u> It's

<u>25.</u> I've

B8   **Practice Exercise**

Word	Synonym	Antonym
over	above on top of	under below
old	aged, oldness olden, decrepit	young, youth infancy

hot	warm thermal	cold frigid
pretty	beautiful lovely	ugly gruesome
far	distant far off, long range	near close
messy	dirty unclean	clean spotless
wet	moist damp, watery	dry arid
high	lofty tall	low level to the ground
long	lengthy lanky	short, brief, curtreduced, curtailed

Practice Exercise

1. beautiful
2. rapidly
3. tasty
4. unsafe
5. near
6. greatest number of
7. most delicious
8. below
9. close to
10. lots of
11. curved
12. pointy
13. sugary
14. transparent
15. not true
16. huge
17. larger
18. tough
19. hot
20. warm

Main Exercise—Story 1

1   important, lots of, terrible
2   types, marine life, dwell, bottom, danger, visitors
3   near to, run into, petrol, confuses
4   ruined, more than, species, around
5   chopped down, plant life, gather at, step on, worst, refuse, gorgeous

Postreading Exercise

1. 5   2. 3   3. 7   4. 5   5. 2   6. 4

Main Exercise—Story 2

6   advantageous, quicker, recycle
7   energy, close the lights
8   reuse things, purchase, produced, discarding it

Postreading Exercise

1. 6   2. 8   3. 7

B9 **A** – The Verb **To Be**

1. (b) **Is** Mike a boy?
2. (b) **Is** Kikkik going home at 5:00 p.m.?
3. (a) Suchera and Cham Chon **are** from Bangkok?
4. (b) **Were** we going to the park?
5. (a) They **were** at the party?
6. (b) **Am** I allowed to go fishing?
7. (a) Toon **is** a great artist?
8. (a) **Were** we playing soccer yesterday?
9. (a) We **are** allowed to water-ski tomorrow?
10. (b) **Are** People from Chiang Mai great artists?
11. (a) Oi **was swimming** yesterday.
12. (b) **Was** Mint sick last week?
13. (b) **Are** Bee and Jobim great water-skiers?

B – The Verb **Do**

1. (b) **Does** Peera **like** to eat pad Thai?
2. (b) **Does** Fung **swim** in the ocean every day?
3. (b) **Did** Sun **eat** her vegetables?
4. (a) **Do you know** Thanadol?
5. (b) It **rains** in Thailand in the summer.
6. (b) **Do** sharks **swim faster** than dolphins?
7. (a) Tata **likes** to water-ski.
8. (a) **Does** the dugong **look like** a manatee?
9. (a) Thai people **like** mangoes better than papayas.
10. (b) For some people, **does** the durian **taste bitter**?
11. (a) Poon **turned off** the computer last night.
12. (b) **Did** Pun **eat** all her dinner last night?
13. (a) Yes, I **ate** all my beans last night.
    (a) No, I **didn't eat** all my beans last night.
14. (a) **Did** the cat **come** home last night?

B10

Animal	Group Name	Action
1. dolphins	a. school	dive, swim, wriggle
2. lions	b. pride	gallop, trot, run, roar, eat, chew
3. squirrels	c. scurry	climb, chew, run
4. birds	d. flock	fly, hover, peck
5. elephants	e. herd	run, trumpet, blow water
6. ants	f. colony	gather, scurry

Practice Exercise 1

waddled	wallowed	strutted	galloped	pecked
soared	gnawed	barked	swallowed	swung
swam	hovered	howled	dove	basked
wallowed	climbed	hooted	thumped	trumpeted

(A) On the Farm with Farm Animals

cackling	moo	singing	chirping	mooing
bahing	cackling	wallow	snort	hooting
barking	gallop	neigh	swimming	waddling

(B) In the Jungle

trumpeting	pride	roaring	swinging
wallowing	fly	hover	dive
chatter	singing	gallops	thump
climb	wriggle	climbs	herd
trumpeting	eaten	croak	hop

B11   Practice Exercise

1. was	2. was	3. were	4. were	5. was
6. are	7. is	8. is	9. were	10. is

The Verb To Be

1. am	2. is	3. is	4. are	5. am
6. are	7. were	8. is	9. is	10. Is

The Present Continuous

1. feeding	2. raising	3. spraying	4. flapping	5. riding
6. riding	7. following	8. leading	9. eating	10. eating
11. playing	12. spraying	13. sipping		

B12   Make your own answers.

B13   Practice Questions

1. how long	2. where	3. whose	4. how long
5. what time	6. when	7. how	8. how long
9. how much	10. how long	11. which	

Main Exercise:

1. <u>Which animal loves to eat sugarcane?</u>
   <u>What animal loves to eat sugarcane?</u>
   <u>What do elephants love to eat?</u>
2. <u>Where is Phuket?</u>
   <u>Is Phuket in the southern part of Thailand?</u>
   <u>Is Phuket in Thailand?</u>
3. <u>How do elephants cool themselves down?</u>
   <u>Why do elephants flap their ears?</u>
   <u>What do elephants do with their ears?</u>
4. <u>What is a tsunami?</u>
   <u>Is a tsunami a wave?</u>
   <u>Where does a tsunami happen?</u>
5. <u>Where is Thailand?</u>
   <u>Is Thailand in Southeast Asia?</u>
6. <u>Is a **wat** a Buddhist Thai temple</u>
   <u>What is a **wat**?</u>
   <u>What is the name of a Buddhist Thai temple?</u>
7. <u>At what time does the sun set in Thailand every day of the year?</u>
   <u>When does the sun set in Thailand every day of the year?</u>
   <u>What does the sun do in Thailand at 7:00 p.m.?</u>
8. <u>Who is the present king of Thailand?</u>
   <u>Who is King Rama IX (or Blumibol)?</u>
   <u>What are Rama IX (or Blumibol) duties?</u>
9. <u>How many people live in Thailand?</u>
   <u>Where do sixty-six million people live?</u>
10. <u>When did the Thai king, Rama IX, celebrate his eightieth birthday?</u>
    <u>Which birthday did the Thai king, Rama IX, celebrate in 2012?</u>
    <u>What happened for the Thai king, Rama IX, in 2012?</u>
11. <u>What happened for King Rama IX in 2006?</u>
    <u>When did King Rama IX celebrate his fiftieth year on the throne?</u>
    <u>What did King Rama IX celebrate in 2006?</u>
12. <u>What can happen to a person who criticizes the king?</u>
    <u>Who long can a person in Thailand go to jail for criticizing the king?</u>
    <u>Why can a person in Thailand can go to jail for seven years?</u>
13. <u>What do most Thais practice?</u>
    <u>What type of Buddhism do most Thais practice?</u>
    <u>What is the most popular religion in Thailand?</u>
14. <u>When was Ayuttyaha Thailand's capital?</u>
    <u>Was Ayuttyaha Thailand's capital before 1757?</u>
    <u>Which city was the capital of Thailand before 1757?</u>

15. <u>What is the Hi-So?</u>
    <u>Are the Hi-So wealthy?</u>
    <u>What is the Hi-So is made up of?</u>
    <u>Are the Hi-So part of the Thai nobility?</u>
16. <u>How do Thais greet each other?</u>
    <u>What is a **wai**?</u>
    <u>Why do Thais bow?</u>
    <u>What do Thais do before they execute a **wai**?</u>
17. <u>How does a person executes a **wai**?</u>
    <u>Why do people clasp their hands together in front of them?</u>
    <u>Where does a person clasp their hands when they execute a **wai**?</u>
18. <u>What is the symbol of Thai Buddhism?</u>
    <u>Who is Buddha?</u>
    <u>Does Thai Buddhism have a symbol?</u>
19. <u>Where do most of Thailand's **monks** live?</u>
    <u>Who lives in wats?</u>
    <u>Do all of Thailand's **monks** live in wats?.</u>
20. <u>How many monks are in Thailand?</u>
    <u>What does Thailand have about 300,000 of?</u>
    <u>Does Thailand have many monks?</u>

B14 **Practice Exercise 1**

1. <u>marks</u>	2. <u>are</u>	3. <u>naps</u>	4. <u>is</u>
5. <u>wants</u>	6. <u>want</u>	7. <u>jumps</u>	8. <u>are</u>
9. <u>is</u>	10. <u>runs</u>	11. <u>giving</u>	12. <u>is</u>

Practice Exercise 2:

1. <u>are</u>	2. <u>went</u>	3. <u>go</u>	4. <u>is</u>
5. <u>am</u>	6. <u>is</u>	7. <u>was</u>	8. <u>is</u>

Main Exercises

1. <u>is</u>	2. <u>is</u>	3. <u>play</u>	4. <u>is</u>	5. <u>is</u>, <u>is</u>
6. <u>sings</u>	7. <u>are</u>	8. <u>is</u>	9. <u>sings</u>	10. <u>is</u>
11. <u>eat</u>	12. <u>is</u>	13. <u>is</u>	14. <u>shopping</u>	15. <u>Is</u>
16. <u>was</u>	17. <u>loves</u>	18. <u>wants</u>	19. <u>taking</u>	20. <u>want</u>
21. <u>is</u>	22. <u>is</u>			

I1   1. It is **Monday, 6:00 p.m.** <u>Talk about what you did, what you are doing, or what you will do on</u> **Monday**.

Note: Noon = 12:00 p.m.

10:00 a.m.   This morning, I **rode** an elephant.

12:00 p.m.	I also **fed** elephants sugarcane and bananas and **petted** them.
1:00 p.m.	In the afternoon, I **took** a bus to Kata Beach.
2:00 p.m.	Then I **relaxed** on Kata beach for a few hours.
4:00 p.m.	In the later afternoon, I **windsurfed** for two hours.
6:00 p.m.	Now, I am **taking** a bus back to Patong Beach.
7:00 p.m.	Tonight I will **eat** octopus on a stick.
8:00 p.m.	In the evening, I will **drink** a big coconut drink out of a coconut shell.

2. It is now **Wednesday**. Talk about what you did on **Tuesday**.

11:00 a.m.	Yesterday morning, I **rented** scuba gear.
12:00 p.m.	At noon, I **went** scuba diving. I **saw** many beautiful fish fish, flora, and fauna on the reef and **took** pictures with a waterproof camera.
4:00 p.m.	I **watched** the dolphins **jump** in and out of the water.
6:00 p.m.	In the early evening, I **ate** a spicy Thai dish of Tom Yam.
7:00 p.m.	Then I **waded** in the cool water.
8:00 p.m.	At 8:00 p.m., I **drank** cold drinks on the beachfront.
9:00 p.m.	Then I **walked** on the beach.
10:00 p.m.	In the later evening, I **listened** to music that **was** being **played** by street entertainers.

3. It is now **Monday**. Talk about what you will do **Friday**.

12:00 p.m.	I will **sleep** in until noon. I will then **eat** spicy Thai food for lunch.
1:00 p.m.	In the early afternoon, I will **rent** a motorcycle, then **ride** around the island of Phuket.
2:00 p.m.	I will **arrive** at the east side of Phuket Island. I will then **tour** the small towns.
3:00 p.m.	In midafternoon, I will **rent** a mask and **snorkel** in the waters of Ko Phat.
6:00 p.m.	At dinner, I will **eat** octopus on a stick and **drink** pineapple juice out of a pineapple.
7:00 p.m.	In the early evening, I will **drive** back to Patong.
8:00 p.m.	After **arriving** in Patong, I will **eat** burgers and fries.
9:00 p.m.	In the evening, I will **walk** on the beach, then **sit** down for a few hours to **take in** the cool breezes from the ocean.

4. It is now **Wednesday**. Talk about what you will do on **Thursday**.

| 10:00 a.m. | Tomorrow morning, I will **shop** at a shopping mall. I will then **have** a pineapple drink out of the shell. I will then **buy** souvenirs. |
| 12:00 p.m. | At noon, I will **eat** lunch on the beach. |

2:00 p.m.	In the early afternoon, I will **rent** a surfboard, then **surf** for a few hours.			
4:00 p.m.	I will **relax** on the beach and **watch** dolphins **play** in the water.			
6:00 p.m.	At dinner, I will **eat** pizza at a pizza restaurant.			
7:00 p.m.	After dinner, I will **go** to Phuket Fantasea, Phuket's theme park, to **watch** acrobats, traditional Thai dancers, and fireworks.			

5. It is now **Friday**. Talk about what you did on **Wednesday**.

9:00 a.m.	In the morning, I **went** on a tour of Krabi. I **saw** many beautiful mountains on the bus ride to Krabi.
11:00 a.m.	In the later morning, I **visited** the Hot Springs waterfall before reaching Krabi.
1:00 p.m.	After lunch, I **went** rock climbing at Railay Bay.
3:00 p.m.	Then I **visited** Wat Tham Sena.
5:00 p.m.	Just before dinner, I **rode** in a glass-bottom boat on Maya Bay. Then I **drank** coconut juice out of a coconut shell. I **saw** beautiful fish swim under the boat. Then I **jumped** into the water from the boat and **swam** for a while.
7:00 p.m.	I **arrived** back on shore in the early evening. Then I **waded** around in the water.
8:00 p.m.	In midevening, I **took** the bus back to Phuket.

I2 **Practice Exercise**

1. PP	2. PPC	3. PC	4. PC	5. PS
6. PS	7. PP	8. PPC	9. PP	10. PS
11. PC	12. PS	13. PP	14. PPC	15. PS

Present Simple

1. ride	2. snorkels	3. fall	4. roll
5. glide	6. climb	7. drink	8. drink
9. ride	10. paraglides	11. Swim	12. lies
13. shines	14. spray		

Present Continuous

1. falling	2. riding	3. flying	4. spraying	5. climbing
6. rolling	7. snorkeling	8. lying	9. sipping	10. jumping
11. drinking	12. riding	13. paragliding	14. floating	15. swimming

I3 **Practice exercise**

5. the	6. the	9. the	10. the
11. the	14. the	16. the	19. the
23. the	24. the U.S.	25. the	

227

14 **Practice Exercise 1**

1. <u>swam</u>   2. <u>sat</u>   3. <u>flew</u>   4. <u>left</u>   5. <u>came</u>

Practice Exercise 2

1. <u>sprayed</u>   2. <u>wanted</u>   3. <u>studied</u>   4. <u>played</u>   5.<u>climbed</u>

Main Exercise

1. <u>ate</u>   2. <u>tasted</u>   3. <u>napped</u>   4. <u>had</u>

5. <u>munched</u> 6. <u>tasted</u> 7. <u>guzzled</u>   8. <u>sipped</u>

9. <u>sipped</u>, <u>waded</u>   10. <u>stopped</u>   11. <u>made</u>   12. <u>woke</u>, <u>laid</u>

13. <u>finished</u>, <u>went</u>   14. <u>made</u>, <u>ate</u> 15. <u>ate</u>, <u>was</u> 16. <u>were</u>

17. <u>went</u>, <u>bought</u>   18. <u>made</u>   19. <u>gets</u>   20. <u>paddled</u>, <u>got</u>, <u>ate</u>

21. <u>offered</u> 22. <u>woke</u>, <u>went</u>, <u>gathered</u>

15 **Practice Exercise**

1. <u>therefore</u>   2. <u>or</u>   3. <u>in addition to</u>   4. <u>but</u>

5. <u>because</u>   6. <u>so</u>, <u>therefore</u> 7. <u>or</u>   8. <u>moreover</u>

9. <u>besides</u>   10. <u>so</u>   11. <u>on the other hand</u> 12. <u>but</u>

13. <u>and</u>   14. <u>as a result</u> 15. <u>for</u>, <u>because</u>

Main Exercise

1. Three of the carriages on the Ferris wheel have two people in them, **but** one carriage on the Ferris wheel has three people in it.
2. The two people are at the same level as the bird; **moreover**, they are feeding the bird.
3. The people in line are being patient, **but** they may haveto wait longer because the Ferris wheel is crowded.
4. The man has a flower in his hand; **however**, he wants to give the flower to the girl.
5. The girl is standing next to the Ferris wheel, **but** she doesn't want to ride it, because she wants the boy to give her the flower.
6. I am afraid, **but (however)** I will be brave.
7. Hold on tight, **because** we'll be down soon.
8. I should not have gone on this ride, **but** I was challenged by Sue to do it.
9. Don't get too close to the fire-breathing man, **because** the fire is spreading.
10. The kids have to move, **because** the fire truck is coming.
11. The man is stuck on the coaster loop, **so** the firemen will have to rescue him.
12. The man should not have climbed on top of the rollercoaster; **therefore** he must be drunk.
13. The man sells popcorn, **and** he sells cotton candy.
14. The popcorn is delicious, **but** it costs too much.
15. The pig is running around freely, **but** it should be on a leash.
16. The man is the pig's master, **so** he should put it on a leash.
17. The fire truck is making a lot of noise, **but** I am happy it is here, because there is a fire.

I6 Practice Exercise
1. (a) keep (b) kept   2. (a) accepted (b) accept   3. (a) ride (b) rode
4. (a) went (b) go   5. (a) returned (b) return   6. (a) didn't (b) don't
7. (a) carried (b) carry   8. (a) drank (b) drink   9. (a) has (b) have
10. (a) sure (b) was sure   11. (a) slept (b) sleep   12. (a) studied (b) study

Story 1

went	is	has	visited	see	saw
riding	decided	go	fulfilled	rode	remember
was	was	was	had	attacked	told
hear	run	stampede	chained	run	chased	be

Story 2

went	were	saw	feed	asked	told
went	bought	went	raised	made	thrust
gobbled	pet	bought	returned	bought	fed
loved	make	were	feeding	enjoying	feeding
went	ask	told	ride	told	thought
got	chained	riding	told	running	startled
stampede	fall	runs	rode	controlling	rode
feel	was	swayed	had		

I7 Exercise
1. like   2. by   3. about, beside   4. without
5. for   6. for   7. of   8. by
9. along, into   10. on   11. from   12. through, with
13. on   14. of   15. with   16. with
17. in, of

Prepositions and Prepositional Phrases
1. **By** is in a prepositional phrase; therefore, it **is** a preposition.
2. The word **down** is **not in** a **prepositional phrase**, so it **is not** a **preposition.**
3. **Along** is in a prepositional phrase; therefore, it **is** a preposition.
4. The word **outside** is **not in** a **prepositional phrase**, so it **is not** a **preposition.**
5. **By** is in a prepositional phrase; therefore, it **is** a preposition.
6. **About** is in a prepositional phrase; therefore, it **is** a preposition.
7. The word **with** is **not in** a **prepositional phrase**, so it **is not** a **preposition.**
8. The word **past** is **not in** a **prepositional phrase**, so it **is not** a **preposition.**
9. **In** is in a prepositional phrase; therefore, it **is** a preposition.
10. **During** is in a prepositional phrase; therefore, it **is** a preposition.
11. **For** is in a prepositional phrase; therefore, it **is** a preposition.

I8   **Practice Exercise**
   1. **sleep**   (a)   I **slept** at 10:00 p.m. last night. _____
                   (b)   My mother **sleeps** on her side. _____
   2. **throw**   (a)   She **threw** the ball over the fence. _____
                   (b)   She **threw** the ball with a sideways spin. _____
   3. **plan**   (a)   I **plan** every move I make when I invest. _____
                   (b)   Mom **planned** our trip carefully. _____
   4. **walk**   (a)   I **walked** quickly through the door. _____
                   (b)   I **walk** with a limp. _____
   5. taste   (a)   I've **tasted** every soft drink, but I like _____
                          ` Coke the best. _____
                   (b)   _____ This food **tastes** bland. _____

Main Exercise
1. A   2. S   3. A   4. A   5. S   6. S   7. A   8. S   9. A   10. A
11. A   12. S   13. S   14. S   15. A   16. A   17. S   18. A   19. A   20. S

I9   **Exercise A**
1. is   2. poss   3. Is   4. Poss
5. Poss   6. Is   7. Poss   8. Is
9. Poss   10. Is   11. Is   12. poss
13. Is   14. Is   15. Poss   16. Is

Exercise B
1. 1   2. > 1   3. 1   4. > 1   5. 1
6. 1   7. > 1   8. >1   9. 1   10. >1
11. 1   12. 1   13. >1   14. 1   15. >1

I10   **Practice Exercise One**
1. since   2. for   3. since   4. since   5. for
6. for   7. since   8. for   9. since   10. for

Practice Exercise Two

1. How **much** danger are we in?
    We aren't in any danger.

2. How **much** ice cream should we buy?
    We should buy **a lot** of ice cream.

3. How **much** pollution is there in the city?
    There's only **a little** pollution in the city today.

4. How **much** sunscreen should we put on?
    We should put on **a lot** of sunscreen.

5. How **much** fluid is in the fluid container?
   There's **a lot** of fluid in the fluid container.

Practice Exercise Three

1. How **many** boys are on each team?
   Each team has **ten** boys.
2. How **many** dresses does your sister own?
   She owns **five** dresses.
3. How **many** phones are in your home?
4. There are **three** phones in my home.
5. How **many** speakers will speak tonight?
   Three speakers will speak tonight.

Practice Exercise Four

1. Much	2. A little	3. Many	4. A few	5. A little
6. Much	7. Much	8. A little	9. A little	10. Much

Practice Exercise Five — Choose the Correct Word

1. (a) since	(b) for	2. (a) many	(b) much
3. (a) much	(b) many	4. (a) many	(b) a lot
5. (a) a lot	(b) one-hundred	6. (a) a little	(b) seven
7. (a) since	(b) for	8. (a) for	(b) since
9. (a) much	(b) many	10. (a) five	(b) much

Main Exercise—Story

1. many	2. for	3. many	4. for	5. many
6. many	7. much	8. many	9. a lot of	10. a little
11. much	12. a lot	13. many	14. many	15. much
16. for	17. many	18. a few	19. a little	20. much
21. much	22. a little	23. since		

I11 Practice Exercise

1. The shoulder **width** of an adult Asian elephant can be up to three meters.
2. A surfboard is two meters **long**.
3. A clownfish can live in waters to a **depth** of hundreds of meters.
4. A dolphin can jump two meters **high**.
5. The tail of a whale is two meters **long**.
6. The edges of an elephant's ears have a **thickness** of a few centimeters.
7. A dugong's body has a **length** of three meters.
8. A mermaid's tail can be one meter **long**.
9. A turtle's shell can be one meter **wide**.
10. Dolphins can swim in waters that are many meters **deep**.
11. A coral reef can have a **length** of many kilometers.
12. A whale can blow water to a **height** of many meters.

Main Exercise

1. (a) Cha Am's beach is forty kilometers **long**.
   (b) Cha Am's beach has a **length** of forty kilometers.
2. (a) The reefs at Ko Phangang are twenty meters **deep**.
   (b) The reefs at Ko Phangang have a **depth** of twenty meters.
3. (a) The standing Buddha on Khao Takiab is twenty meters **high**.
   (b) The standing Buddha on Khao Takiab has a **height** of twenty meters.
4. (a) The shoulders of an Asian elephant are three meters **wide**.
   (b) The shoulders of an Asian elephant have a **width** of three meters.
5. (a) The solid gold Buddha, Wat Chedi Sao, **weighs** 1,507 kilograms.
   (b) The solid gold Buddha, Wat Chedi Sao, has a **weight** of 1,507 kilograms.
6. (a) Doi Suthep Mountain is 1,676 meters **high**.
   (b) Doi Suthep Mountain has a **height** of 1,676 meters.
7. (a) The Kinnaree statue's torso is several meters **long**.
   (b) The Kinnaree statue's torso has a **length** of several meters.
8. (a) The fine white sand beach at Ko Tao is 2.5 kilometers **long**.
   (b) The fine white sand beach at Ko Tao has a **length** of 2.5 kilometers.
9. (a) Wat Phra That Cho Hae's gilded chedi is thirty-three meters **high**.
   (b) Wat Phra That Cho Hae's gilded chedi has a **height** of thirty-three meters.
10. (a) The pointed Chedi of Nakhon Pathom is 127 meters high.
    (b) The pointed Chedi of Nakhon Pathom has a **height** of 127 meters.
11. (a) The Emerald Buddha at Wat Phra Keo is a few meters **high**.
    (b) The Emerald Buddha at Wat Phra Keo has a **height** of a few meters.
12. (a) Paragliders at Hua Hin Beach can soar in the air hundreds of meters **high**.
    (b) Paragliders at Hua Hin Beach can soar in the air to a **height** of hundreds of meters.
13. (a) Chedi, Wat Thammamongkhon is ninety-five meters **high**.
    (b) Chedi, Wat Thammamongkhon has a **height** of ninety-five meters.

I12 **Practice Exercise**

1. (e)   2. (f)   3. (i)   4. (b)   5. (d)   6. (h)   7. (a)   8. (c)   9. (g)

Practice Exercise

1. myself   2. herself   3. yourselves   4. herself
5. themselves 6. Itself   7. himself   8. yourself
9. ourselves   10. themselves 11. himself   12. yourself

Essay

1. himself	2. yourselves	3. himself	4. herself
5. itself	6. themselves	7. themselves	8. yourself
9. themselves	10. himself	11. yourself	12. themselves
13. myself	14. ourselves	15. themselves	16. herself
17. itself	18. myself		

I13 **Practice Exercise**

1. powerful	2. powerfully	3. enchanting	4. quickly
5. gracefully	6. slowly	7. strongly	8. strong
9. calm	10. calmly	11. slowly	12. brightly
13. great	14. intensive	15. ideally	

Main Exercise

1. beautifully	2. amazingly	3. beautiful	4. royal
5. royally	6. gracefully	7. stylish	8. appealingly
9. ancient	10. deeply	11. tightly	12. entirely
13. generously	14. powerful	15. heavily	16. beautifully
17. enchanting, gracefully		18. originally	19. traditional
20. traditionally	21. quickly	22. gracefully	23. grand
24. virtuous	25. virtuously		

I14 **Modals Practice**

1. must (have to)	2. allowed	3. might	4. should
5. must	6. should	7. have to (must)	
8. should	9. have to (must)	10. ought to	

Practice Exercise

11. had to	lack of necessity	12. should	advice
13. would you	assistance	14. could	ability/permisssion
15. must not	prohibition	16. should	suggestion
17. had to	necessity	18. shouldn't	advice/suggestion

Main Exercise:

1. should	suggestion	2. had better	advice
3. should	suggestion	4. could you	assistance
5. should	suggestion	6. should	suggestion
must	necessity	must	necessity
7. shouldn't	suggestion	8. can	ability
must be	logical		
9. shouldn't	suggestion	10. must not	prohibition
must not	prohibition	shouldn't	suggestion

11. should	suggestion	12. shouldn't	
must	ability/conclusion		suggestion/advice
might	conclusion	must not	prohibition
13. must not	prohibition	14. cannot	inability
cannot	inability		
15. must/have to	necessity	16. shouldn't	suggestion
should	necessity	must not	prohibition
17. shouldn't	suggestion	18. has to be	necessity
19. shouldn't	suggestion	20. have to	necessity
21. should	advice	22. cannot	inability
23. should	suggestion/advice		

A1 **Practice**

<u>Noun</u>: **elephant** <u>Adjective</u>: **big**
   <u>Adjective clause</u>: that was really big and majestic

1. <u>Noun</u>: **sunset** <u>Adjective</u>: **gorgeous**
   <u>Adjective clause</u>: that was amazingly gorgeous and spectacular

2. <u>Noun</u>: **elephant** <u>Adjective</u>: **big**
   <u>Adjective clause</u>: which was big and amazingly powerful

3. <u>Noun</u>: **beach** <u>Adjective</u>: **beautiful**
   <u>Adjective clause</u>: that was beautiful and had blue sparkling water

4. <u>Noun</u>: **island** <u>Adjective</u>: **big**
   <u>Adjective clause</u>: that is big and that has many beautiful beacheswith sparkling blue water

5. <u>Noun</u>: **ornaments** <u>Adjective</u>: **beautiful**
   <u>Adjective clause</u>: that are shiny, majestic, and amazingly beautiful

6. Noun: **pottery** <u>Adjective</u>: **lovely**
   <u>Adjective clause</u>: lovely and gracefully crafted

7. <u>Noun</u>: **floating market** <u>Adjective</u>: **bustling**
   <u>Adjective clause</u>: that was bustling with a heightened sense of excitement

8. <u>Noun</u>: **longboat** <u>Adjective</u>: **magnificent**
   <u>Adjective clause</u>: that was enchanting, majestic, and magnificently adorned with special ornaments

9. <u>Noun</u>: **triggerfish** <u>Adjective</u>: **beautifully striped**
   <u>Adjective clause</u>: that was glowing and beautifully striped swam by us.

10. Noun: **Tom Yam dish** <u>Adjective</u>: **spicy**
   <u>Adjective clause</u>: that was flavory and spicy, and whose bouquet captured all noses

The Hindu Influence in Thailand

1. Hinduism was brought to Thailand by **settlers** who had **Mon** ancestry.
2. Mons and Khmers were influenced by **merchants** who were derived from **Hindu** heritage.
3. Thai kings based their laws on **law codes** derived from the ancient and scholarly **Hindu** codes of law.
4. Brahman priests still conduct **rituals** based on the prominent and culturally derived **Hindu** style.
5. In 1431, King Trailok adopted **artwork** based on magnificent **Hindu** artistic styles.
6. Thai kings still base some ceremonies on **rituals** adopted from mystical, legendary, and ancient **Hindu** rites.
7. Thai dance is still based on **performances** originating from ancient legends of Ramayana ideals of culture and arts.
8. The Ramakien is the Thai version of the story of the **Rama gods** and their inspirational and heroic feats.
9. The Ramakien has been turned into a **drama** that is chock-full of gracious and graceful **dance** moves.
10. There are 174 **paintings and murals** beautifully painted from the motif of **Ramakien** artwork.
11. The Emerald Buddha Temple has many **paintings** originating from the stylistic interpretations of **Ramakien** art.
12. The Ramakien has also been made into a **puppet show** with puppets crafted from **interesting** and stylish characters.
13. The puppets are made from **buffalo skins** that are **stretched** tightly across the skillfully crafted puppet forms.
14. The puppets represent **characters** sourced from varied and **different** representations of the Ramkien gods.

A2   Practice Exercises
1. **Will** Prang **be going** to Phuket tomorrow?
2. **Must** Kanoon **do** her homework tonight?
3. **Should** Prim **be arriving** soon?
4. **Will** Tiger **be absent** from school today?
5. **Is** Toon **used to studying** every night?
6. **Did** Haddis **play** soccer a lot before?
7. **Has** Pao **been practicing** her singing every day?

Main Exercise
1. **Are** many crocodiles **prowling** the rivers close to the rain forests?
2. **Can** creatures like the fiddler crab **climb** trees to catch their prey?

3. **Have** mangrove trees in the forest **been able** to withstand the annual floods by using their own complex root systems?
4. **Must** mangrove trees **trap** nutrients and soil with their roots for food?
5. **Have** requirements to survive in the forest's ecosystem **produced** many different variations or types of organisms in a single species?
6. **Must** anyone going into a forest **be** careful, because there are a lot of wild elephants and tigers walking in there?
7. **Can** any animal **be eaten** by other animals in the forest?
8. **Have** over two hundred tree species **been growing** in Thai forests for years?
9. Does Thailand **host** 10 percent of the world's fishes?
10. **Are** mud skippers **able** to walk on the mud to chase prey?
11. **Have** insects **been adapting** to the harsh jungle in order to survive?
12. **Have** animals in the lower areas of the forests **survived** better than in the upper hills?
13. Must plants in lower forests **be able** to regularly shed their leaves?
14. **Have** over two hundred species of trees **been identified** in each acre?
15. **Will** monkeys **call** out to each other to warn of incoming predators?
16. **Will** wild animals **be able** to survive due to conservation efforts?
17. Do jungles **become** very noisy when the sun comes up?
18. Do a lot of animals in the forest **have to come** out after dark, because they cannot bear the fierce heat of the jungle?

A3 **Practice Exercises**
A 1. c 2. e 3. b 4. g 5. a 6. i 7. f 8. h 9. d
B 10. k 11. l 12. j

Main Exercise—Ko Samui Story
1. The most prominent feature is a jagged headland of rock that separates the Chawaeng and Lamai Beaches.
2. There is also glistening-white sand on the beach.
3. A jagged headland of rock separates the beaches of Chawaeng and Lamai.
4. Na Thon is the name of the primary port on the island of Ko Samui.
5. The village of Na Muang is lined with lots of trees.
6. Many jungles are on the hills of Muang.
7. The waterfall at Na Hunag is breathtaking.
8. The waterfall at Na Huang is 105 feet high.
9. The beautiful butterflies of Samui Butterfly Gardens have a lot of different colors, with a kaleidoscope-filled assortment.
10. There isn't a lot of space to move around at Bophut Beach because it is quite narrow.
11. The beaches next to Chawaeng have fewer people on them because they are less developed and have fewer hotels and restaurants on them.
12. Emerald-green water surrounds the caves at Mu Koh park.

A4 **Practice Exercises**

(1) Subject +   verb
     Teachers   teach.
     Teachers   talk.
     Teachers   lecture.
     Students   learn.
     Students   study.
     Children   play.
     I   eat.
     I   laugh.

(2) Subject +   verb +   object
     Teachers   teach   students.
     Teachers   teach   arithmetic.
     Teachers   teach   English.
     Teachers   talk   to students.
     Students   learn   math.
     Students   learn   from teachers.

(3) Subject +   verb +   indirect object +   direct object
     Teachers   teach   students   English.
     Teachers   give   students   tests.
     Teachers   talk   _____   _____.
     Teachers   talk   _____   _____.
     Students   learn   _____   _____.
     Students   _____ _____   _____.

(4) Subject +   verb +   complement
     Teachers   are   educated.
     Teachers   are   dedicated.
     Teachers   are   _____.
     Students   are   innovative.
     Students   are   eager to learn.
     Students   are   innovative.

Main Exercise
(1) A Monkey Climbing a Tree

(1) Subject +   verb
     Monkeys   run.
     Monkeys   climb.
     Monkeys   eat.

(2) Subject +   verb +   object
     Monkeys   eat   bananas.

237

Monkeys	climb	trees.
Monkeys	like	bananas.
Monkeys	love	climbing.

(3) <u>Subject</u> + <u>verb</u> + <u>indirect object</u> + <u>direct object</u>

People give	monkeys	bananas.
Monkeys give	people	joy.
Monkeys give	each other	bananas.
People give	monkeys	peanuts.

(4) <u>Subject</u> + <u>verb</u> + <u>complement</u>

Monkeys	are	cute.
Monkeys	are	tree climbers.
Monkeys	are	curious.
Monkeys	are	primates.

(2) A Girl Riding an Elephant

(1) <u>Subject</u> + <u>verb</u>

Elephants	play.
Elephants	herd.
Elephants	spray.

(2) <u>Subject</u> + <u>verb</u> + <u>object</u>

Elephants	eat	bananas
Elephants	carry	people.
The girl	rides	elephants.
Elephants	blow	water.

(3) <u>Subject</u> + <u>verb</u> + <u>indirect object</u> + <u>direct object</u>

People	give	elephants	bananas
People	give	elephants	fruit.
Elephants	give	people	rides.
Elephants	give	people	joy.

(4) <u>Subject</u> + <u>verb</u> + <u>complement</u>

Elephants	are	enormous.
Elephants	are	massive.
Elephants	are	intelligent.
Elephants	are	ungulate mammals.

(3) An Elephant Eating Bananas

(1) <u>Subject</u> + <u>verb</u>

Elephants	eat.
Elephants	play..
Elephants	trumpet.

	(2)	Subject +	verb +	object
		Elephants	eat	bananas.
		Elephants	flap	their ears.
		Elephants	love	bananas.

(3)	Subject +	verb +	indirect object +	direct object
	People	give	elephants	bananas
	Elephants	eat	bananas	from trees.
	Elephants	pick	bananas	off trees.

(4)	Subject +	verb +	complement
	Elephants	are	enormous.
	Elephants	are	fruit lovers.
	Elephants	are	banana eaters.

(4) A Dolphin Jumping through a Hoop

(1)	Subject +	verb
	Dolphins	jump.
	Dolphins	swim.
	Dolphins	eat.

(2)	Subject +	verb +	object
	Dolphins	eat	fish.

(3)	Subject +	verb +	indirect object +	direct object
	People	feed	dolphins	fish.
	Dolphins	give	people	pleasure.

(4)	Subject +	verb +	complement
	Dolphins	are	cute.
	Dolphins	swim	in the ocean.
	Dolphins	love	swimming.

A5 Practice Exercise: Nouns

1. tribe   2. pelts   3. rattan   4. jute
5. headdress 6. ancestors 7. rite   8. ritual

Practice Exercise: Adjectives

1. primitive 2. fond

Practice Exercise: Adjectives + Nouns

1. silver studs   2. fringed headdress   3. evil spirits
4. monsoon season   5. medicinal plant roots 6. silver-studded jackets
7. aembroidered costume 8. nipah palm leaves   9. edible roots

Practice Exercise: **Verbs**

1. lurk 2. build 3. surround 4. vibrate
5. gather 6. stretch 7. swing 8. perform

Practice Exercises: **Phrasal Verbs**

1. pressed close 2. adhere to 3. keep away

Questions

1. <u>What do the Mlarbi women do with bamboo leaves?</u>

The Mlarbi are sometimes called the <u>"People of the Forest"</u>. The Mlarbi women gather vegetables and fruits from the forest, but they also gather different types of **leaves** and fruits from the forest to make household goods. One special thing the women gather is **banana leaves**. The women use the banana leaves to build new homes. They wait until the banana leaves turn yellow and dry out before using them. Thai people sometimes call the Mlarbi <u>the "Spirit of the Yellow Leaves"</u> because the Mlarbi use banana leaves to build their homes.

2. <u>Do the Mlarbi own TVs or computers?</u>

No, the Mlarbi do not own any modern electrical appliances. The Mlarbi live in huts in the jungle, so they do not have electricity in their homes. The Mlarbi also move often, so they do not have access to electricity.

4. <u>Names some things that Thailand's tribes do to protect themselves from evil spirits.</u>

The women perform special rites and rituals to protect themselves from evil spirits. These include wearing neck rings, swinging on ropes for three days, and wearing special clothes and costumes. The women also pray to their ancestors while they perform these rituals.

5. <u>How do the women of the Ahha tribe celebrate New Year's?</u>

The women of the Ahha tribe celebrate New Year's by swinging off trees for three days. They do this to make sure the crops grow well.

6. <u>Do northern Thai tribes buy their clothes at shopping malls?</u>

No, all the women make their own clothing. The women of all tribes are fond of using beads, silver, seeds, monkey fur, and chicken feathers to make embroidered costumes, amulets, jackets, bags, and headdresses. The women wear all this special clothing, even when they are not performing ceremonies.

7. <u>What do women in various Thai tribes do to decorate their clothing and their household goods?</u>

The women of the Meo and Acha tribes wear special headwear. Women in the Meo, Acha, and Yao tribes make specialized embroidered costumes, amulets, jackets, bags, and headdresses. The women of all tribes are fond of using silver, seeds, coins, monkey fur, and chicken feathers in their creations.

8. <u>What do you think of the brass neck rings the Padaung women wear?</u>

I think that it would hurt to wear the neck rings, so I don't like it that these women wear them. The rings are also very rigid, so it seems that the women cannot move well because of the neck rings.

240

9. <u>What special name is given to the Mlarbi people, and why?</u>
The Mlarbi people are called People of the Forest because they build their homes from banana leaves. When the leaves dry out, the Mlarbi then have to go back into the forest to gather more leaves, so that they can build new homes again.

A6   <u>Practice Exercise</u>: <u>**Nouns and Adjectives**</u>

1. rampart   2. merchant   3. irrigation
4. intricate   5. opulence   6. ruins, idyllic

<u>Practice Exercise</u>: <u>**Verbs**</u>

1. founded   2. proclaimed   3. waned, abandoned
4. converge   5. restored

<u>Practice Exercise</u>: <u>**Hyphenated Compound Words**</u>

1. D   2. E   3. B   4. F   5. H   6. A   7. C   8. G

<u>Practice Exercise</u>: <u>**Un-hyphenated Compound Words**</u>

1. B   2. G   3. A   4. F   5. E   6. D   7. C

<u>**Essay**</u>

1. pre-eminent   2. golden age   3. temple-building
4. well-thought-of   5. township   6. leftover
7. downturn   8. ransacked   9. super-huge
10. upstream   11. man-made   12. well-to-do
13. downstream   14. ruined-nature   15. old-fashioned

A7   <u>Practice Exercises</u>: <u>**Nouns**</u>

1. B   2. C   3. A

<u>Practice Exercises</u>: <u>**Adjectives + Nouns**</u>

1. C   2. B   3. I   4. D   5. E
6. F   7. A   8. H   9. J   10. G

<u>Practice Exercises</u>: <u>**Phrasal Verbs**</u>

1. B   2. A   3. E   4.   5. H   6. J
7. I   8. L   9. F   10. K   11. D   12. C

<u>**Exercises from the Story**</u>

(1) unscathed   corpses   wildlife
(2) pin down   get crazy   tipped them off   pick up
(3) bringing about   spread out
(4) ran for   scatter away   move up
(5) screen it out   going on   works out

A8   <u>Practice Exercise</u>

1.   I swam in an ocean **<u>whose</u>** water was warm.
2.   I rode an elephant **<u>that</u>** swayed back and forth as it walked.

3. The dugong is a strange-looking animal **that** lives in the ocean.
4. The dolphin is a mammal **that** swims very fast.
5. The crocodile has sharp teeth **whose** bite is dangerous.

Main Exercise
1. Bangkok is a big city **that** has a lot of shopping malls.
2. Chang Mai is a charming city **that** attracts a lot of tourists.
3. Ayuttyaha is an ancient city **that** has a lot of ancient temples.
4. Ko Phangan has a beach **that** is famous for its full-moon party.
5. Ko Phangan also has some coral reefs **that** are full of beautiful fish.
6. Ko Phi Phi Don and Ko Phi Phi Ley are twin islands **that** both have beautiful beaches.
7. Hat Khlong Khong is a beach **that** is famous for its snorkeling.
8. Many tribes **that** live in Northern Thailand mostly live in the mountains.
9. Doi Inthanon is Thailand's highest mountain.
10. James Bond Island is a famous island **where** James Bond filmed a movie.
11. Market Chatguchak is a market **that** is the world's biggest flea market.
12. Samut Prakan has a crocodile farm **that** is home to fish and crocodiles.
13. The crocodile farm has a shop **that** sells crocodile skin handbags and shoes.
14. The crocodile handlers wrestle crocodiles **that** are dangerous.
15. Ko Chang is a beautiful island **that** is Thailand's second largest.
16. Khlong Chao is a waterfall **that** attracts many visitors.
17. Khao Wang is a huge palace **that** was the summer residence of King Mongkut.

A9   Match nouns or noun phrases with their definitions:

| **A** | 1. C | 2. B | 3. A | 4. E | 5. D |
| **B** | 6. G | 7. J | 8. H | 9. I | 10. F |

Phrasal Verbs

1. M	2. C	3. J	4. F	5. H	6. I	7. L
8. Q	9. O	10. G	11. K	12. A	13. P	14. E
15. N	16. B	17. D				

Story

1. come from	2. bring about	3. presented with	4. dug up
5. packed full of	6. takes place	7. takes in	8. strewn throughout
9. put up	10. carried out	11. takes place	12. shaved clean
13. attend to	14. shaved off	15. put on	16. bless them with
17. made up of			

A11   Practice Exercises (A) Present Perfect
1. I have been studying at this school **for a long time.**
2. There's been less traffic in Bangkok **since** they built the subway.

3. I have lived in Chang Mai **for many years.**
4. The Thais have been practicing Buddhism **for centuries.**

Practice Exercise (B) Present Perfect Continuous

1. I have been studying at this school **for four years.** _____.
2. I have been studying at this school **since** _____.
3. I have lived in Chang Mai **for sixteen years** _____.
4. I have lived in Chang Mai **since** _____.

Main Exercise

1. PPC	2. PP	3. PPC	4. PP	5. PP
6. PPC	7. PPC	8. PPP	9. PPC	10. PPC
11. PP	12. PP	13. PPC	14. PP	15. PPC
16. PP	17. PPC	18. PPC	19. PPC	20. PPC
21. PP	22. PPC	23. PPC	24. PPC	25. PP
26. PPC	27. PP	28. PPC	29. PP	30. PP
31. PP	32. PP			

Story Thai Kings and Thai History

(1) PPC PP (2) PP PPC (3) PPC PPC PP
(4) PPC PP PPC (5) PPC PP PPC (6) PPC PPC PPC

A12 Compound Word Definitions

Motor scooters	small vehicles that are powered by a motor
fuel-efficient	refers to motorcycle or car that do not use much gas
multifaceted	something that has many uses, or a person that has many skills
well-to-do	refers to a person who is rich or has lots of money
heavily congested	refers to a road that is full of vehicles
often-seen	refers to something that occurs very, very often
overrun	refers to something that has an excess of something
danger-prone	a situation, or a person, that is likely to be dangerous
breastfeed	refers to a mother who feeds her child naturally
taxi-men	men who operate motorcycles as a taxi
low-cost	a thing that does not cost a lot of money to operate
well-marked	something that is very easily seen or noticed
well-defined	something that is very clearly obvious
cycle-propelled	refers to a vehicle that is operated by people, especially when they have to pedal to provide power for the vehicle
people-powered	a vehicle that gets its power from the exertion of a person and not an engine

243

run-down	refers to something that is so tattered, old, or worn out, or no longer usable
out-of-date	refers to something that is old and ancient andthat is not used anymore
awe-inspiring	refers to something that is so very, very wonderful and amazing
premodern	an older, less modern form of something
elephant trekking	to ride atop an elephant on a long journey
self-propelled	a vehicle that is not powered by a motor but that is powered by a person, such as a bicycle
must-see	something that is so incredibly wonderful that it must be seen and not missed
meat eaters	a person or animal that eats meat
well-known	famous, familiar to many people
engine-powered	a vehicle that is propelled by an engine
odd-looking	something that looks strange or out of the ordinary
well-built	something that is of high quality because it is built so very well
third-class	refers to a form of travel or transportation that is the third best
first-class	refers to the best form of travel or transportation

A13 Example Exercise

(a) The clownfish is a beautiful, small fish.
           1   2   3

(b) The clownfish is an exotic-looking, small, striped fish.
                1   2   3   5

(c) The clownfish is a strange-looking, striped, Thai fish.
              1   2   5   6

(d) The clownfish is an orange-faced fish.
               1   2

(a)–(d) The clownfish is a beautiful, exotic, and strange-looking,
                1   2   2   2

orange-faced, small, striped, Thai fish.
      2   3   5   6

Main Exercise

1. The Puffer Fish

The puffer fish puffs itself up, so it can have a big, round belly.
                                                 1   2   3

1. (a) The puffer fish is <u>a</u> <u>big-bellied</u> fish.
           1   2

   (b) The puffer fish is <u>an</u> <u>exotic-looking</u>, <u>gray</u>, <u>Thai</u> fish.
           1   3   5   6

   (c) The puffer fish is <u>a</u> <u>hideous</u> fish.
           1   3

2. **Crown of Thorns Starfish**
   (a) The crown of thorns starfish is <u>a</u> <u>headless</u> fish.
           1   3

   (b) The crown of thorns starfish is <u>a</u> <u>multicolored</u> fish.
           1   5

   (c) The crown of thorns starfish is <u>a</u> <u>spiky</u>, <u>unsightly</u>, <u>pink-and-white</u> fish.
           1   3   3   5

3. **The Dugong**
   (a) The dugong **looks like** <u>a</u> <u>small</u>, <u>marine</u> elephant.
           1   2   3

   (b) The dugong is <u>a</u>, <u>big</u>, <u>friendly</u>, <u>herbivorous</u>, <u>marine</u> mammal.
           1 2   3   3   3

   (c) The dugong is <u>an</u> <u>odd-looking</u>, <u>gray</u> mammal.
           1   2   5

4. **Bottlenose Dolphin**
   (a) The bottlenose dolphin is <u>a</u> <u>svelte</u>, <u>quick-swimming</u> fish.
           1   3   3

   (b) The bottlenose dolphin is <u>a</u> <u>beautiful</u>, <u>gray</u> cetacean.
           1   3   5

   (c) The bottlenose dolphin is <u>an</u> <u>oval-shaped</u>, <u>cetaceous</u> fish.
           1   2   3

5. **Scorpion Fish**
   (a) The scorpion fish is <u>a</u> <u>poisonous</u>, <u>spiky</u> fish.
           1   3   7

   (b) The scorpion fish is <u>a</u> <u>mean-looking</u>, <u>orange-colored</u> fish.
           1   3   5

   (c) The scorpion fish is <u>an</u> <u>ugly</u> fish.
           1   3

6. **The Cuttlefish**
   (a) The cuttlefish swims quickly with its <u>powerful</u> <u>dorsal</u> fins.
           3   5

   (b) The cuttlefish is <u>a</u> <u>beautiful</u>, <u>cetaceous</u>, <u>multicolored</u> fish.
           1   3   3   5

   (c) The cuttlefish's head is <u>round shaped</u>, <u>bright</u>, and <u>multicolored</u>.
           2   3   5

7. **the lagoon triggerfish**

   (a) the lagoon triggerfish is a long, multicolored fish.
                         1 2   5

   (b) the lagoon triggerfish has a yellow lip and a long, oval-shaped head.
                        1   5   1 2   2

   (c) the lagoon triggerfish has a long, oval-shaped, multicolored
                            1 2   2   5

   body, with two thin flippers.
                  2

A14   Nouns, Verbs, Adverbs, and Adjectives

1. C   2. D   3. B   4. A   5. F   6. G   7. E

Phrasal Verbs

1. G   2. D   3. H   4. I   5. C   6. A   7. E   8. B   9. F

Idiomatic Phrases

1. C   2. D   3. L   4. F   5. A   6. K
7. I   8. E   9. J   10. G   11. H   12. B

Writing or Speaking Exercises

1. C

2. The government decided to stop the abuse of the forests and took actions to ensure the survival of wilderness areas.

3. Adorning its hilltop refers to one wat on the mountain, while dotting them describes how many waterfalls are on the mountains. Adorning its hilltop is also more descriptive and describes things in a more beautiful, enchanting way.

4. **Wonders of nature** talks about beautiful things that happen naturally, while **human-inspired wonders** are not natural and are built by humans instead.

5. (c)

6. When the water falls down, it creates noise and turbulence. This is similar to the hectic city life of Bangkok. After that, the water flows into serene pools, which represent the serene nature of Thai Buddhism. When people bathe in the waters, they can link the two polar opposites of city life and Thai Buddhism together and find a balance between them.

7. (e) pay respect to the mountain, and to the spirit of the mountain

8. Adorn is used as a beautiful, descriptive word. It tries to give the impression that the Buddha statues and the wat make the places that they are put in more beautiful, more enchanting, more lovely.

9. Previously hidden means that many beautiful places could not be reached before and could therefore not be seen by Thai people. After some trees were sawed down and after roads were built, and after Thai people started buying and using automobiles more, they could then visit, see, or live in beautiful areas that could not be reached or seen before.

Printed in the United States
By Bookmasters